RULE BREAKERS

Changing the Way Actors Do Business

BY VALORIE HUBBARD

CEO ACTOR'S FAST TRACK

Copyright © 2017 Valorie Hubbard and Actor's Fast Track

Rule Breakers: Changing the Way Actors Do Business
By Valorie Hubbard
CEO Actor's Fast Track

All rights reserved. No part of this book may be reproduced, stored in a retrieval system or transmitted by any other means without the written permission of the publisher and author.

ActorsFastTrack.com
ISBN: 978-0-9897049-8-4 (print book)
ISBN: 978-0-9897049-9-1 (ebook)]

Cover design by O'Daniel Designs

Interior text design and printing by Gorham Printing

Printed in the United States of America

Legacy ONE
AUTHORS

Kirkland, WA

www.legacyoneauthors.com

I dedicate this book to actors, the ones who are determined, talented, and magical. I love my work and I love my clients. Actors, this book is for you guys!

I am dedicated to you understanding that each of you are an entrepreneur and your acting business is your call. It's time to create your own system for breaking the rules. Enjoy this book.

Love, Valorie

FOREWORD

I grew up in a very small, isolated town in northern Canada. While there weren't many outlets—actually, none—I had always had the acting bug. When I was 16 on the advice of Dame Judi Dench, with whom I had a life changing chance encounter, I applied to film school in Los Angeles. It was a summer program and they were very selective with their applicants. Much to my excitement and disbelief I was accepted. I packed my suitcase and was on a flight to LA.

Upon arrival, the first course I took was a scene study class. I wasn't quite sure what to expect, but once the instructor walked in and began speaking I instantly felt like I had made the right decision. The instructor was Valorie Hubbard and it was seven years ago (2010) when I met her. Valorie has served as a mentor and friend to me since the first day of classes. I instantly felt a degree of trust with Valorie that I hadn't encountered in any previous acting class. I had been taking acting workshops for a while and spent well into the thousands of my parents' hard earned money. The one thing I kept pondering was why the individuals offering classes weren't out doing what they were teaching given that they had the "keys to guaranteed success."

Valorie was different in that she had a resume a mile long of major film and television credits and was practicing what she was preaching. Still to this day, what she teaches remains one of the most valuable lessons I ever received. I am a product, a commodity.

If you're an actor reading this, then you too are a product. What so many actors fail to realize is that in this industry, we are not employees. Each of us are a company that has a unique brand. Therefore, we need to know more than just how to bring a character to life. We need to know how to operate a business so we can bring our company and our career to live, as well. Valorie made me understand this important truth.

Corporations spend millions of dollars and several years trying to ascertain their target demographic, determine their mission and goals, and develop quality branding that attracts their perfect clients. As an actor, success requires that you do those things, too. Yes, I understand how stressful that seems to digest. I had a little panic attack when I was first introduced to the notion that, as an actor, I was running the company of me. Suddenly I felt like I was in a fantasy that was far beyond my reach. However, Valorie taught me what to do. She has the tools and first-hand experience that helped me turn that fantasy into a reality.

Valorie's approach to acting is the most useful and practical one I have ever encountered. I recall one of her first lessons was on achieving goals. She used the example of wanting to win an Academy Award. She said, "so you want to win an Oscar. That's not an unattainable goal, you just need to know the steps to get there. To win, you need to be nominated. To be nominated, you need to have a leading role in a major feature film. For that, you'll need the experience and resume to be noticed, which means that you need to be known to casting directors, producers, and directors working on the mainstream projects. It's much easier to get in those meetings if you have a reputable agent. To get that agent, you need to know how to sell yourself."

From that very first class seven years ago, Valorie taught me the importance of knowing how to market and sell myself and my unique brand to my consumers—the television and film powers who would one day cast me.

Granted, not everyone can head off to Los Angeles for the summer. Yes, there are a great number of obstacles standing between where you are now and getting on the other side of the television screen. But, Valorie gave me the foundation to do it. I still live in Canada, currently in Calgary, Alberta, which has an astounding amount of talent and some major productions. But, it is by no means Los Angeles or New York City. With Valorie's help, I'm proud to say that I am one of the few people who can make a living solely in the film industry. I have Valorie to thank for never having to wait tables while I pursue my dream because she taught me how to start my business on the right path and avoid the pitfalls.

I have worked on everything from ultra-low budget indie films to scripted network television. With every job, the key to my success was knowing my brand and how to sell myself. I have Valorie to thank that insight.

—David Oulton

CONTENTS

Foreword ... 4
Acknowledgments ... 8
Introduction ... 9

Product Development: Branding and How To Do It Right ... 19

Chapter 1   Create An Irresistible Product: Brand Yourself ... 21
Chapter 2   How To Develop Your Brand ... 29

Marketing: Attract Buyers By Applying Business Principles To Your Career ... 33

Chapter 3   Know Your Key Buyers ... 35

Increase Your Sales and Get The Audition ... 43

Chapter 4   Be A Constant Seller ... 45
Chapter 5   Pitch Yourself To Buyers ... 55

Business Mindset and Competitive Advantage: How To Stand Out In the Crowd and Leap To Success ... 75

Chapter 6   Mindset Determines Your Success Or Failure ... 77
Chapter 7   Plan Your Competitive Advantage ... 91
Chapter 8   Overcoming The Ten Obstacles All Actors Face ... 103

                Cast: In order of appearance ... 116
                About the Author ... 120

ACKNOWLEDGMENTS

Thank you to the following amazing people:

Dad—for giving me your entrepreneur spirit. I miss you so much.

Mom—for everything. You are the best for sure. Thank you for your organization and your willingness to keep moving forward. Go Mom!

Gill—for being the love of my life, my best friend, and partner in crime.

Tina—for running the show big time.

Karen Lynn Maher—for your expertise guiding me through the writing and publishing process—and Catherine Lenox for your words. And, for all the fun.

To my coaches: Michele Scism, Melissa McFarlane, Jay Perry, James Hallett, and Belanie Dishong. Thank you for your amazing guidance.

I love all my Actor's Fast Track clients, students, coaches, and former clients.

To my friends and family, I wouldn't be here without your continued support.

If we all loved each other, wouldn't it be a beautiful world? We are all in one boat together, from me to the smallest child in Syria and Africa. All in one boat. Our main interest should be the love and care of each human being and of each other. As the American spiritual teacher, Ram Dass said, "We are all just walking each other home."—Valorie Hubbard

INTRODUCTION

Why this book? Because it is not like all the other myriad "how-to-break-into-Hollywood-or-Broadway" books on the market. Within its pages are the proven, bold approaches I've used to build my own successful acting career.

I offer a radically different approach to booking theater, TV and film roles which will most likely stretch your comfort zone, and I'm sharing it because it works.

Why write it now? Because I'm driven and inspired by the belief that no talented, serious actor should *ever* be left behind. And I am the *only* working actor taking a lead in the industry to change how actors get hired. I want to give you a better, faster way to get work.

Too often actors unwittingly get in the way of their brilliant success. It's not your fault. You've merely followed instructions you've been given from a broken system. My system gives you viable, new instructions that produce results. By following the methods in this book, you will get work.

In short, you'll discover how to become your own solution. The system I've created frees you from following the crowd and puts you out in front. It literally fast-tracks your career.

I teach what I teach because it works. It's not rocket science, but it is akin to magic. Quite simply, if you follow my instructions, your career will change.

And that's when the magic begins!

If you're looking for a traditional read that will tell you "how-to-get-an-agent" or if you're only interested in amateur community theatre, you may as well put this book back on the shelf. ***It is for serious actors only***.

If you want a book about getting an agent, then go to my friend K. Callan. She writes the New York and LA agent books and really bears down on the subject. I will have no hard feelings.

But if you're tired of getting stuck in part-time roles or never hired as a series regular and want to be a full-time actor, this book will give you a plan of action to leap beyond those frustrating plateaus into the right rooms and get hired for the roles you want.

Here, I present a unique system for serious actors who want to get noticed and paid for full-time, professional work. If you're willing to be courageous, tenacious, and savvy to get work, then his book is for you. It will teach you how to break "the rules" and land substantial roles on your own.

Committing to being a full-time actor can be very frustrating and often hard on your self-esteem. Sometimes it seems like a break will never come your way, no matter how hard you work at it. You've submitted your headshot, resume, and cover letter to multiple projects but still aren't getting auditions for the roles you want to book.

Or even if you do get auditions, you're not getting hired. Your friends and family may push at you to quit. And you may have even thought of quitting yourself.

If I ask ten actors, "What are you doing about your career?" most will tell me, "Well, I'm waiting to get new headshots, I'm looking for a new agent, I'm thinking about taking this or that acting class."

This is a recurring theme. I see it repeatedly. They are **waiting**! FOR WHAT? They don't have to wait. And neither do you! You can change it. You can activate. Stop waiting! There's plenty to do that doesn't include sitting and waiting for something to happen.

At first, I was going to give you my top ten actor mistakes and solutions to getting the career of your dreams. However, you can already get this as a gift from me if you opt into my website, actorsfasttrack.com.

Then I decided to share my technique for success. Nowhere else is there a blueprint for a career in the arts or a guide for how to build your successful acting career. I initially narrowed my methods into a fun, accessible little iBook which you can find on iTunes. https://itunes.apple.com/us/book/id1124771654

However, as I thought about this book, I realized I wanted to give you much more because you'll need the information in it to succeed. Here, I delve much deeper into how to accelerate your life and acting career.

My overriding goal for this book is to turn actors into "perfect business entrepreneurs" because I believe if I put a bunch of smart actors out there, it's bound to have an impact on how hiring is done in the industry and will help professional actors get hired more quickly and agents make more money.

Curious? Interested? I've discovered how to do it, so you can too.

If you're truly committed to pushing your career ahead quickly and to following the advice in this book, together we will get you there.

How? Read on.

In the product development section of this book, you'll learn:

- How to brand your identity or character type and the roles most suited to you.
- How to maintain consistency of that brand and get noticed and hired as a professional actor.

Next in the marketing section, you'll discover:

- How to identify and develop outreach strategies for getting connected to your buyers—the people in charge of hiring you. You'll learn who they are and how to get their attention.
- How to take what you've learned in previous chapters and put it into action to get yourself into the marketplace.

Further on in the sales section of the book, you'll learn:

- Why selling what you offer is essential to your success.
- When and how to make sales calls.
- How to land an audition and get hired.

Finally, in the mindset/personal development section, you'll master:

- Ways to bypass boundaries set by others, be confident and get the role you know is right for you.
- Awareness of how your mindset may be sabotaging your success and how to change it.
- Techniques for getting out of your own way, including guidance from Actor's Fast Track coaches.
- What it means to be in competitive advantage and why it is such a powerful support to your career.
- How to achieve the big results you want—and continue to achieve them.

Thought-provoking exercises at the end of each chapter will also give you the opportunity to look at where you are in your own career and where you can make changes to move it forward more quickly.

Overall, you'll learn:

- How to strategically define your brand.
- How to form a solid marketing and sales plan.
- How to develop a buyers' outreach strategy.
- How to find and influence those crucial business relationships that will book you work.
- How to let go of fear to be successful.
- How to manifest your dream of becoming a professional actor through proven methods.

Doing this will distinguish you from the crowd of myriad other want-to-be actors. It is the single most important aspect which separates those who succeed from those who don't.

Throughout the book, you'll also read firsthand accounts from my clients— actors who, like you, wanted to fast-track their careers but didn't know how to do it. You'll discover the steps they took to leap over the hurdles they faced when trying to get work. You'll share in their struggles and their successes. You'll learn how to follow in their successful footsteps.

One of my friends, Peyton McDavitt says, "There are those who do and those who do not." Congratulations for deciding to read this book! You are a "doer."

Among doers, of course, there are many variations. But nonetheless, you are in league with the likes of Meryl Streep and Daniel Day Lewis. Hooray! Bravo! You are actively doing something about your career. I fully agree with Peyton.

Through this book and my coaching, I will be your acting "Sherpa," helping you navigate what feels like Mount Everest and giving you the guidance, air and tools needed to reach the top. You'll have to lace up your acting boots to join me as we forge together to the top. But trust me, when you follow my guidance, you'll be able to leap ahead over any boulders that stand in your way.

Hang on, because it promises to be a craggy, wild climb. But if you stay with me, success is definitely within your reach.

I've launched thousands of talented actors' careers and helped guide them through the Hollywood and New York morass because I'm also in the thick of it. And it's been a blast. Let's go claim the career of your dreams together!

Forging Through the Mind Saboteurs: How I Became a Successful Working Actor

What if your life depended on your acting career and you'd starve to death if you just waited to be discovered?

I wish I'd had someone ask me this when I first got into the business! It could have spared me some tough pitfalls in my thirty-year acting career. But no one did, which is why I'm here for you now.

As one of the top ten percent working actors in Hollywood today and owner of the company *Actors Fast Track*, I consult daily with working actors about their career paths and ask this pertinent question of anyone who walks in my door who wants to fast-track their career.

Why? Because to become a successful working actor, it's critical they change their mindset about how they view the impact and value they bring to their work. To move their careers from part-time work into full-time roles, actors must have a single-mindedly focus on that goal.

In my first book, *The Actors Workbook: How to Become a Working Actor*, published by Allyn Amp Bacon Publishers, co-written with my dear friend and filmmaker Lea Tolub-Brandenberg, I taught readers how to transition from student acting to professional work.

This second book teaches professional actors to move beyond being stuck in small, low-profile roles to booking visible, full-time work. This distinct method is a result of new thoughts, mindsets and actions that have been working successfully for me and my clients.

To give you a more complete understanding of how I'm able to help actors be successful, a look at my background is useful.

Acting has always been my passion. And it is FUN! I was born to act. Always given to dramatizing with a flourish, my first acting performance was at the age of three when, much to my mother's dismay, I dramatically flung myself down a staircase because I'd seen an actress do it in a movie. Horrified, she thought I was dead and sent my dad to the basement stairs where he found me quite alive and laughing. Once my relieved parents saw I wasn't dead, they promptly enrolled me in a creative dramatics class where, ostensibly, my zest for drama would not be so dangerous. I've been acting ever since.

My career has led me through performing at the New Jersey Shakespeare Festival, Delaware Theatre Company, The Wilma Theatre, Weston Playhouse, Missouri Rep and The Lab Theatre in Poland, where I was a member of the last international company to work at the Lab Theatre. My background also includes work with the amazing professionals John Guare, Joseph Chailken, Toni Kotite, Neel Keller, Terry Schreiber and Zbigniew Cynkutis. Needless to say, moving to Los Angeles brought about a huge change when I launched into screen work.

My film credits include *Sex, Death and Bowling; Trigger; A Better Life; An American Christmas Carol; Divorce Invitation; The Hannah Montana Movie; Smell of Success; Pennance; Resident Evil: Extinction; Parasomnia; Henry Fool; Wrestling with Alligators; Gameday;* and the Hallmark Christmas movie *Help for the Holidays.*

Television credits include roles on *Castle, Agent of S.H.I.E.L.D; How I Met Your Mother; Glee; American Horror Story; Workaholics; True Blood; 90210; ER; Desperate Housewives; The Middle; Zeke and Luther; Good Luck Charlie; I'm in the Band;* a recurring role on *Kickin It and General Hospital; HUGE; The Job; Missing Persons; Comedy Central; American Body Shop* and *Chocolate News.* I also play "hot" Rhonda in the video game *Dead Rising 3.*

Plus, while it's not truly acting, my roles as wife of Chef Gill Boyd and mother to our dog, Gracie, are among my favorites.

Since you are already an actor, I'm going to ask you to imagine for just a minute you could wake up every day as a working actor, that your day was super busy with auditions, fittings, lunches, classes, and that every day was about YOU and your dream of acting. You could confidently call yourself an actor and others would see you that way!

Guess what? That is exactly what my days look like now. And what my clients' days look like too. And the reason? It's because I run a great business. I'm an acting entrepreneur. And they don't teach that in acting school. The teachers there work to help you develop your talent but they don't explain that if you want to be successfully paid for full-time work, acting is your business.

This is a very important concept and central to this book, so it's worth repeating: ***Acting is your business.***

When I graduated from acting school at the Goodman School of Drama thirty years ago, now the Theatre School of DePaul, I went straight to New York with an agent. As it turns out, the agent was more interested in bedding my then actor husband than helping me with my career. The agent told me I didn't have name recognition to get the roles I wanted and that I needed more roles before he could do anything for me. This was not a good start.

I struggled along by myself with NO direction and NO idea how to get to where I wanted to go. All I knew is I wanted to make money as an actor and I wanted to be a movie star, but I had no idea how to make that happen.

Despite going to a big acting school, I wasn't told when I graduated that I was now an entrepreneur and owner of a small business. I wasn't told this because the acting school didn't know it either. And when statistics say 80 percent of small businesses fail in the first two years, what were my chances going to be for success if I didn't even know I had a business?

As great luck would have it, I found the wonderful Jay Perry and his company, Actors Information Project (now, regrettably no longer in business!) Jay literally changed my life and my career. He taught me how to build my career as a business and go after it with fervor on a daily basis. He showed me how to boldly step into my career. And I have had a blast!

When I was 40 years old, enthused by the idea of working on the big screen, I moved to Los Angeles. I was dismayed to learn I had to start all over again. WHAT!? I'd had New York credits! But it didn't matter. Plus, there were five times as many casting directors in Los Angeles as there'd been in New York. I was so overwhelmed! It felt as though everything I tried had a roadblock, "actors can't do this or that."

But here was the deal and the reason I didn't perish in the maelstrom: Jay Perry had taught me that my acting career was a business, and he'd taught me well. I knew if I could be successful in New York City, I could replicate that success in Los Angeles.

So when my agent told me I didn't have the name to get work, I made a plan and hired a career coach. And, yes! I marched right to casting on my own and got the role! The next thing I knew, I was hired on *How I Met Your Mother, Workaholics, True Blood, Resident Evil,* etc.

As I became more and more successful, I started to notice great actors around me were falling on their proverbial asses and tragically giving up their dreams. I knew I could help these people because I understood the dynamic that underscored getting exceptionally great work.

I know what it means to be a struggling actor. It's hard, discouraging, and even scary at times. But it's my mission to change the world and the way actors get work one actor at a time.

You may be thinking, *"I've done something like this before and it didn't work."* Or you may have worked with someone who you think did something akin to what I'm doing. This could be true, but I'm here to say **I know I am the only working actor out here offering a system to help other actors get hired.** I've seen firsthand how other folks are playing by rules that are rigged against us. To fast track our dream careers, Actor's Fast Track offers a unique, dynamic way to get hired quickly in the roles you want. It's changing the way actors do business. And it's driven by our own rules.

I have worked as an actor my entire life. And I still do. My clients sign up to work with me over and over again because I support them 100 percent. Their success is as important to me as my own. And, because I treat them as individuals, they each get exactly what they need on their own level.

I advise them to be sure they are ready to change. If you're seriously not willing to tell people you're an actor, then stop trying to be an actor. You're getting in the way of those of us who are serious about our careers! In other words, stop getting in MY way.

"But I'm too old to get out there," you may tell yourself. Wrong.

I have a 55-year-old client who just booked a co-star role on a TV show. Now she's primed to work with a number one agent who specializes in co-stars. Because my client has already booked a co-star role, she can go into the room, look that agent right in the eye and say, "Look, I'm back in the game. I figured out how to book a co-star on my own. I'm yours for the taking. You and I are the perfect match."

I've also worked with a 70-year-old actor. You are never too old to realize your dreams.

"*I **am** serious about acting, I'm just not ready to get out there*," you may object. "I need to go to a real acting school first!" No, you don't. Guess who else didn't go to acting school? Johnny Depp. So you can take that excuse for not fast-tracking your career right off your list.

The truth is, we are never really "ready." If you're waiting to be ready, stop waiting! It's okay. You are as ready as you'll ever be. So, be available. If you truly believe you need to "be ready," it's time to look for another career.

But, if you are willing to "be ready," it will help you break that self-defeating cycle. Stop listening to the naysayers who say you can't do it or those who convince you in any way you're not ready for it. Are you going to live your life or let someone else live it for you? No one can commit to YOU better than you. And trust me: There is enough chocolate cake for everyone.

Actors don't have career paths clearly defined for them. Acting schools don't provide graduate school or entry-level positions like many other professions. You may be highly talented, but there's no guarantee your talent alone will get you where you want to go.

The blissful days of being "discovered" are GONE! And merely getting an agent doesn't mean you made it. An agent is just a tiny part of the equation.

To be truly successful actors, we need to muster up the courage to take our career into our own hands. We must understand that we are entrepreneurs and, as such, in business for ourselves. Our talent is what we sell, so we must turn ourselves into the most marketable version of our own product. This means taking complete charge of our own lives.

Think of your acting career as a business in which you are the company. The elements or "departments" you'll need to build for your success are product development, branding, marketing, sales, and finance.

When I coach my clients, I ask them, "*Are you sitting around waiting to be discovered?*" If the answer is yes, I tell them they're dreaming. It's not going to happen. Even if you have an agent, he/she won't ever work as hard for you as you'll work for yourself. Your agent has many people just like you. You're at the top of your list, but only one of many on an agent's list.

Acting is very serious work. At Actor's Fast Track we approach our customers with a truthful assessment of where they are. We help them get grounded, real, and purposeful, and we treat their careers as a business. We assist them in realizing an acting career is not made of inconsequential fairy tales. And while it is inspired by dreams, it only becomes reality through a lot of hard work, planning, strategy, smart thinking, and a heap of courage and drive.

You're an actor! It's not magic or "being found" that builds your success. WORK launches careers. If you're serious about this life role, now is the time to act!

PRODUCT DEVELOPMENT: BRANDING AND HOW TO DO IT RIGHT

CHAPTER 1

CREATE AN IRRESISTIBLE PRODUCT: BRAND YOURSELF

The first step to selling yourself as an actor is to identify and create your brand. Think about yourself as a saleable product. Make your brand consistently unique. This will give you your marketability. In other words, buyers will want to hire you because you will have something specific and unique to offer them that no one else does. Notice that I did not say you need to know YOU, I said you need to know YOUR BRAND—the unique product others see—which will underscore your marketability, so you can sell your product: *YOU*!

What is a brand?

- Your brand is your **essence**. It's how you're seen in the world and what you present to others on a day-to-day basis.
- The best brands deliver **one** concise, clear message that connects immediately with buyers, motivates them to buy, inspires repeat business, and builds customer loyalty.
- Finally, a brand is the **authenticity** you deliver to your customers and a combination of all the experiences they have with you; it is distinctly and uniquely you.

What does it mean to brand yourself as a full-time, professional actor?

- Your brand is the image you choose for yourself and how you are perceived by your audience, agents, managers, casting directors, the media, and anyone else who sees you and your work.

- The goal of branding yourself as an actor is to persuade buyers to hire you and keep doing it because you offer them something unique they can't get elsewhere.

- You can present yourself in whatever light you want to; just be consistent in what you decide you want others to see.

- Specify to yourself which characters you want to play. Say, "This is who I am." Then don't deviate from that decision.

- What you present visually through social media, your headshot, resume, drop-offs, emails, letters, publicity, public relations and anything else that includes your face, credits or behavior should support and market this choice.

- Your brand is also your behavior, which should be so strongly defined that anyone viewing it knows exactly what you want them to see.

- Present yourself in the same way you would if you were selling a specialty product.

- Then go out and confidently sell yourself to buyers.

When I taught acting for years, I always said, "Specific acting is good acting." It's the same with the business of acting.

Too many times actors wait for an agent or manager to show up and tell them who they are. Or they ask me, "What do you think I am?" I can't tell you who you are or what roles are best for you. Nor can an agent or a manager. You must decide that for yourself.

How? It's very simple. To decide how to define your brand, ask yourself:

- What do you want those hiring you to see?
- How do you want to be perceived by the public?
- Who's getting the parts you want right now?

Being an actor is analogous to being an entrepreneur, which means you'll have to build your business from the ground up. Branding is the best place to start.

My client, Mary Somers, says when she moved to L.A. two years ago, spending more money than she'd like to admit on all kinds of headshots, she kept asking herself, *"What's not working?"* Her conclusion mirrored what many actors believe: *"It must be my headshot."*

Mary explains how working with Actors Fast Track has shifted her mindset as an actor.

> *"When I met Valorie, the helplessness I'd been feeling began to slip away. I was unclear about my look and type until she said, "Oh, my god, it's so obvious! You are the BAD girl, the werewolf girlfriend. You're the edgy, bitchy girl. You're not mean, but you have an attitude. You're rough around the edges and don't give a crap." Valorie gave me a consistent direction, shed light on how much is within my control, and taught me that deliberate movement makes a difference."*

Actors often think they need to morph themselves and change their label every time they want to get work when the opposite is true. They need to choose who they are, plant their flag in the sand and say, "This is who I am" and keep saying it over and over again so people will want to buy it.

But actors tend to try to please every customer they meet by changing who they are, and they don't understand that getting hired starts with choosing a brand for themselves and sticking to it, regardless.

Imagine this: You own an Italian restaurant and I come in as your customer and say, "Oh, gosh! You know what? I want Mexican food." And then you say, "Oh, hold on a second; let me go back in the kitchen. Okay, we're cooking Mexican food now."

This is what actors do. They try to please every customer they meet by changing who they are. Instead, we should be the ones who are telling others how to sell us! We are ultimately who decides what our marketability is, not someone else.

Remember the scene in which Dustin Hoffman plays a difficult, temperamental actor in *Tootsie* when the casting director says, "You're too short for the role" and Dustin's character hollers beseechingly, "But I can be tall!?" Viewers laugh because the idea that Dustin was willing to morph himself into anything, including being tall, when he was perceived as being too short for the role was hilarious to the audience. But, in truth, this desperate moment is all too familiar to actors and reflects how some can and often do respond to auditions all the time.

When Dustin Hoffman's character creates who he is and brands himself as *Tootsie*, he not only gets work, he becomes a super star. This is brilliant because that's how it works. Hoffman's character breaks all the rules by recreating himself into a saleable product (a sassy, opinionated woman even though he is truly a man) and springs right past all the naysayers to success.

Actors need to understand that if people don't know what they're buying, they'll never buy it. So you'll need to decide who you want to be and manifest it. This doesn't mean you shouldn't take a branding session or get help from Actor's Fast Track to identify your brand. By all means, do. I highly recommend getting help in identifying who you want to be. We help people get specific.

The first step in branding is to get very clear about what you're selling.

You wouldn't just open a bicycle shop and hope people would buy your bicycles. You would advertise what you have to offer and highlight all the unique aspects about your bicycles that make them more desirable than your competitor's bicycles.

In this same way, package *yourself* as a saleable product. Know your brand. Only then will you understand what you can offer to buyers.

You may be thinking by now, "But, Valorie, how do I find *my* brand? I could spend the rest of my life trying to figure out who I am!"

The distinction I'm making here is straightforward. I'm not asking you to figure out your innermost psychology and feelings as a person. What I am saying is you need to figure out what you do better than anyone else out there and what will be your fastest path to getting hired. Clearly identify what that is, make a plan/platform, and go **book it right now**.

When I see a movie or TV show or a play and there's a part that's right for me, I say to myself, "Oh, I could have done that." Every actor I know does that. This is key to understanding your brand.

For example, I met a kid in Houston who said, "I can't get out." Then he gave me his business card and it had 15 photos of him dressed as 15 different characters. He wasn't getting hired because nobody's going to hire a guy who can do 15 characters. He hadn't branded himself, so it appeared to buyers as though he was nothing unique.

For me, almost every part I play is one of those middle-class people that think they're better than you. I also do Southern very well, and passive-aggressive and evil, mean women, too. I can go to super dark places. I've done that my whole life. I'm very good at evil, scary women. And nosy, gossipy women. In *Bewitched*, I would have been Gladys Kravitz.

I'm the buoyant, ballsy broad who will take you through the fun house—a cross between Kathy Bates and Drew Barrymore. I tend to play the woman that lives across the street from you, and when you see me coming with a casserole, you turn off your lights and pretend you're not home. I'm almost always the comic relief.

If you look at actors, you'll notice the best ones have a brand.

For example, if you hire Russell Crowe, you know you're going to get a brawly kind of rough-around-the-edges guy that'll kick your ass. He's a little scary. He can play someone mean. But if you hire Tom Hanks, you're going to get everybody's friend, everyone's dad, and an understanding guy. Right?

If you look at any working actor today, you can see their positioning statement right away. But people get caught up in the intricacies and say, "Oh, but sometimes I play this person and that person." But I say, "These people you play all have the same characteristics, and they're all the same type of character." Find that common denominator and you've identified your brand.

The problem is, actors want to show variety because that is what they've been told they should do, but being everything for everybody doesn't work.

The real objective is to be able to talk about yourself as a distinctly unique product to anyone who asks. Define for yourself exactly what role you are most suited to and stick to that role definition.

My client and Actor's Fast Track coach, Brian Majestic, is an ace around branding. He's identified who he is and what roles are right for him, and he goes out and gets them.

Brian says, *"I'm the blue-collar, everyman, but I also just know who I am. I finally know what I'm about and not about—where I fit in and where I don't. As an actor and a human being, that's incredibly freeing because it makes me feel more comfortable connecting with others. I'm one of the guys. If I'm a police officer, I'm the one you want to arrive on the scene who's going to take charge and make sure everything's going to be okay."*

Another one of my clients who is very clear about her brand and unstoppable is Esme Banuelos, from Wichita, Kansas. She's had three callbacks to the Hulu show, *East Los*. She put herself on tape for *Chicago Med* on NBC, and she did it all by pitching herself on the phone. She explains:

> *"I want to be an action star. The next Angelina Jolie or Michelle Rodriquez. So, since I want to be an action star, I need to show it in the way I live, let people see that, and let that come out from me.*
>
> *I'm very clear about what I am selling; I'm a tough friend. If there's a boy who's giving you trouble, call me. I will handle it. I'm the person my friends can count on, the person they'll come to first if anything happens. I am also Latina. It's what I am. My parents are first generation. I grew up in a ghetto-like area. Drive-bys happened there."*

Stay unique.

Rather than run all over the place trying new things, stick to your brand and stay the course. Your talent is your product, so you need to showcase it in the best way possible. This includes knowing your strengths and weaknesses and pinpointing the roles that best suit your strength. The clearer you are with your product, the quicker you're going to get hired.

HOW TO BRAND YOURSELF

VALORIE'S LAST MINUTE THOUGHTS:

Here are some great action steps you can take to identify your brand. You don't have to do them all.

- Think of your ideal role. Then, either on your own or with a group of people, brainstorm a list of adjectives that describe you and the kinds of roles you want to book. For example: Ditsy. Smart. Sexy. Goofy. Ballsy. Sultry. Sweet. Tough. Lazy. Grumpy. Earnest. Evil. Write them down.

- Watch TV. What character can you see yourself playing and why? Find the actors who are already booking the parts you want. This applies to theatre, commercial and film. Choose up to five character types you know with certainty are perfect for you. Don't try to be everything to everybody.

- Notice the actors who are getting similar parts right now to determine what the market wants. Who is your competition? Watch what they wear, what other kinds of characters they've played, and write down as many adjectives as you can think of to describe these characters.

- Ask yourself, "What role did I play when I really knocked it out of the park? What roles do I see myself playing or could have seen myself play?" Maybe there was someone in a movie where you thought, "That's my part!" In other words, what role could you walk right out of your house and book? If you saw a role in the breakdowns, which one would inspire you to say, "Oh, that's my role!"

A few more bonus ideas:

- Go shopping.
- Get some clothes to fit the look of your brand.
- Stick to the roles for which you are most suited and dress for that role at auditions.
- Get a graphic designer to design a logo or color scheme that's just right for you.
- Then go be the "you" you've created

> *"I'm a young Jane Adams meets Kimmi Schmidt with a pop of Minnie Driver. I'm the hardworking nursing resident who's holding the family together, caring for her disabled grandparents. I've also been described as a young Carol Kane or Geraldine Hughes."* —**Carolyn Faye Kramer, actor/Actor's Fast Track coach**

Chapter 2

HOW TO DEVELOP YOUR BRAND

Start by getting a professional head shot.

The most immediately visible piece of your packaged product is your headshot. This is your logo. And it's the first thing casting directors see before deciding whether to book you. So when planning your headshots, above all, prepare, prepare, prepare!

Here are some tips you need to consider:

- Casting is done digitally now, so agents are looking at closer shots now more than ever. Think "postage-sized" pictures.

- This is **not** a place where you want to cut corners or be cheap. So don't do it! If you're serious about your career and playing with the big boys, invest in photos that will communicate your level of commitment and professionalism.

- Present yourself in a polished way in your resume and headshot because if you send casting directors an amateurish resume and old, crummy photo, guess what? Whether it's true or not, you've just told them you're an unprofessional actor and you'll be better off to go back to community theatre and get out of this market.

- This is **your** session, not the photographer's. Be specific about what you want in your photo to convey your brand.

- A professional headshot is essential if you truly want a successful acting career.

- Once you know what it is you're selling, your "brand," it is much easier to get a dynamic headshot that will attract the roles you want.

- Know first what you're selling.

- For the sake of preparation, build your character from the shoes up. But remember that you're only going to be seen from the collar of your shirt and above.

- Get plenty of rest before a shoot.

- Choose four current TV, film, theatre or commercial characters you can play. Decide what they'll wear and what they'd be saying. Give each character at least four lines of dialogue so you understand their character better. This will give you three or four looks.

- Research different photographers in your area and choose three or four that photo the kind of pictures that match your "brand-self."

- Don't try to be everything or you will be nothing!

- For each setup, be intentional in your thinking. Remember, you're an actor, so your pictures should be **engaged** and ***active in the eyes.***

- Then go pick a photographer.

Leading with a spectacular headshot can get you the job. I'm thinking about a very good, solid actress I worked with, Taylor Graves. Taylor's headshot was of a pretty girl with brown hair that looked like every other girl. The pictures she was using were "safe." Bland.

But she had this one photo that was unique, different. When I saw it, I said, *"This is it!"* She started using that photo on Facebook and the image was so strong, people started to know her just because of it. Now she uses it for everything. In the year and a half since I've worked with her, she's always in an important play with important people in New York City. She's becoming a well-known, highly regarded theatre actress there. That photo is "the root of Taylor." It's her brand.

Once you have your headshot, here are more steps you can take to develop your brand.

- Get a Pinterest account. Search for brand and business cards to pin to your account so you can get an idea of fonts and colors you may want to use.
- Create Facebook pages.
- Create a business card, postcard and marketing materials.
- Make reels/clips and a website.
- Work with acting coaches/advisors.
- Write a compelling resume.

What should you include on your resume?

- **List your affiliations;** union affiliations are important.
- **Television:** List the role type: Series Regular, Recurring, Guest Star, Co-Star or Featured (a nice word for extra or background).
- **Film:** Again, they want to know the size of the role. Some of the terms you can use here are Lead, Supporting, Principal, Day Player, and Featured. The director is listed in your third column.
- **Theatre:** List your character in the middle column and then the theatre, or the director, or both in the third column.
- **Training:** If you don't have any credits, the next thing they are going to look at is where you were trained.
- **Skills:** What skills are going to get you work? Accents, sports, singing, weaponry, other languages, etc.
- **Contact:** How can I get in touch with you? If you're new to an agency and don't know how reliable they are, make sure your own number is also on the resume.

Remember: this is YOUR career, *not* your agent's career. The resume, reel, postcards or business cards, and your website collectively tell who you are.

Build your business with the right mortar.

Too many times actors do a lot of this stuff that doesn't equate to anything because they don't understand that there's a building and it's called *Their Business*. And everything needs to fit within that same building. It's like someone who doesn't realize they're decorating an entire house. They decorate one room at a time without thinking about how each room fits with the plan for the whole house.

> *Valorie has helped me figure out what I am. As CEO of my own company, my job is to let people know what I am. It's not helpful to market myself as an attractive, talented actress because everybody in L.A. is an attractive, talented actress. She's helped me hone in that I'm a greasy, homeless, street runaway. Zeroing in on this working class, edgy runaway does take me out of getting high school hot girl cheerleader parts. But that's not what I'm chasing down on my end. When I stop trying to be everything, I can be who I am."* —Courtney Bandeko, actor/Actor's Fast Track client

Buyers don't buy what you do—they buy how you do it. So while it's okay to fit in, it's far better to stand out. Make everything you do a personal signature; then "write it" with a flourish!

Actors need to think of their careers as well-branded businesses and apply all the same marketing principles a small business does to attract customers. Think about what you can **bring** to the table, not what you need to get. Be confident and creative in how you define yourself.

> *"Actor's Fast Track gives you the tools to figure out where you fit best in the industry to initially get yourself out there, distinguish yourself, and determine your essence, marketability and strongest assets as a performer."* – Sara Banerjee, actor/Actor's Fast Track client

MARKETING: ATTRACT BUYERS BY APPLYING BUSINESS PRINCIPLES TO YOUR CAREER

CHAPTER 3

KNOW YOUR KEY BUYERS

All successful business owners know that buyers are the lifeblood of their business. Without customers, there's no one to buy their products. And without anyone to buy their products, they are soon out of business.

Who are actors' buyers?

In the business of acting, the buyers are producers, directors, casting directors, and writers. Once you've branded and packaged yourself, you're going to need to start building key relationships with **these** people because they are the ones who are going to pay you to act. You don't need to know everyone. Just a few.

In this chapter, what you'll start building is a list of buyers you want to target so you will be prepared to move forward into the next chapter on selling.

What are some misconceptions about how to reach out to them?

As an actor, you have probably been taught that the path to success is like being on a ladder. The Holy Grail of work is positioned at the top and you, as an actor, are on the bottom. The only thing lower than you is dirt.

To climb the ladder, you believe you first need to join the union and get an agent. Then your agent will introduce you to a manager. The manager will lead you over the invisible line that runs between buyers and sellers to the casting director who will introduce you to the director, writer, and producer. And then, magically, you will get hired.

Believe me, this is one approach, but not the best one.

Focusing on joining the union and getting an agent before you book anything doesn't make any sense. Who you need to pay attention to initially are the buyers/customers who are going to hire you. Know that buyers and ultimately the public are the people whose attention you want to get.

> *"It's more important to me now to meet casting directors than agents. My agents and managers are my team, but I always aim toward the buyers. Before working with Valorie, I understood that I was a product and that managers and agents were sellers, but I didn't know how all of it worked. She made it clear to me that I had to focus on the buyers, not the sellers."* —Ana Maria Perez, actor/Actor's Fast Track client

What is the best way for actors to reach buyers?

It goes without saying casting directors are the first people to lend a hand when it comes to you getting paid work. They are the people who open the door for you to get in front of those who will pay you because this is how that side of the business works. In other words, if I'm making a movie, I hire a casting director to cast it for me. The casting director prequalifies the actors who he thinks could play the part. Actors are selected at auditions. But this doesn't mean the only way you can get in is by using the front door.

Note that a lot people use the incorrect terminology here. You may hear people refer to "casting agents." There is no such thing. The term is "casting director." This confusion of terms prompts actors into thinking an agent is going to get auditions for them. This isn't true. Casting directors manage auditions.

What an agent does is submit your picture to casting directors along with a thousand other pictures for every role that comes out. Then the casting director chooses who they want to see. In other words, all an agent does is push a button to submit you. Everything is done electronically now.

> *"As I started working with Valorie and really developing my niche and marketability rather than bouncing against the wall to see what would stick, she helped me hone in on who I was and what I was going for. She helped me realize the sky is the limit if you take action and put yourself out there in a more direct way."* —Sara Banerjee, actor/Actor's Fast Track client

How to Get Known by Buyers

Once you have identified your brand and know the types of TV, film, play, or commercial roles you are right for, then you need to find out who the people are that are involved in these shows: the casting directors, directors, producers, and writers.

Make a list of ten Casting Directors who cast roles you've already identified as your brand.

1. _____
2. _____
3. _____
4. _____
5. _____
6. _____
7. _____
8. _____
9. _____
10. _____

Make a Hit List

Your next step will be to develop a who/what/how list I call "The Ultimate Hit List." Every one of my clients has one.

When you have your hit list ready, start hitting them. Figuratively speaking, that is! You'll learn more about how to do that in Chapter Four.

As you also go through this process, you'll be knocking on a lot of doors and making a lot of contacts. So it's important to keep the following in mind:

- Be organized; keep accurate records.
- Identify who is casting/directing a project you want to be booked in.
- List the project and details you know about it.
- Gather names of everyone you want to notice you.
- List their addresses, phone numbers, email addresses, and social media outlets.
- Write down how/when/where you met them.
- Enter **every** communication you had with them: when it was and what was said and done in it.
- Include the approach you plan to take to get the attention of the person/people doing the hiring.

This hit list will be with you for your entire career. It's a way to catalogue who you know. And It will **never** be complete until you are done acting.

It's good to start by dividing the names you collect into casting directors, writers, producers, directors and others. Also, add "miscellaneous" because a lot of times in a long career you might meet someone who is a friend of the family and has connections. One actor I know has built his entire career on connections with show runners and camera men.

I learned a great buyers' outreach strategy from my original life coach, Jay Perry. He's a very well-known, highly respected coach. He was friends with Thomas J. Leonard, a major figure in the development of personal coaching. Leonard was an Erhard Seminars Training (EST) employee in the 1980s and founded Coach U, the International Coach Federation and, as an accounting manager, founded the International Association of Coaches.

Jay Perry had a company called the "Actors Information Project" and he taught me, "The Fan Club Game." Below is a chart showing how the game is played.

STRANGER	AWARENESS	PEN PAL	AUDITION	CALL BACK	HIRE	FAN CLUB
Document a lead here when your buyer is a total stranger.	Chart here when you've reached out and developed an initial awareness about a stranger. And while you're not completely sure they know who you are, you're getting your picture and/or video in front of them.	In this phase, document when you've started to make a real connection with a buyer—you get confirmation they do know who you are. You've now become "active" to them. And a great component of this phase is it gains you an audition—because that's what comes next! Your lead becomes responsible for getting you an audition.	The final phase of charting is where the best action begins! You get called in for an audition.	You get a call back to come in for another audition.	You get hired for a role!	In this phase, a director, casting director, producer or writer is doing a project with a part in it that's perfect for you, and you're among the first five to ten people they think of bringing in.

My client, Courtney Bandeko, says discovering she didn't need an agent, manager or rep to get work was a huge shift for her.

> "I was unrepresented and my resume had films on it that I'm really proud of. But it was hard to get people to watch them because they were micro-budget films and reenactment television. Just basically the things you could get through Actors Access without an agent."

Working with Valorie, I was doing outreach, outreach, outreach. And then I booked a movie: Adolescence. Even the director asked how I got the role because I didn't have an agent. I had full faith in Valorie and her process, but to actually get a job from the work she had me do was awesome."

You are the best advocate for yourself.

To fast-track your career:

- Identify who hires your brand.

- Focus on getting connected to these people through a variety of outreach activities.

- Believe unwaveringly that your brand is right for the roles you want.

- Understand that casting directors who are looking to buy what they view as a consistent, unique product. They are the people you want to attract with your brand

"Be unafraid to see yourself as a solution to the casting director's problem. Instead of thinking, "Oh, my god, am I annoying these casting directors when I reach out to them," know you're there to solve their problem. They need someone to fill a role and do it well. They need you to take the work on the page and do it better than what's there—do the part and bring it to life in an exciting way. It's okay to be self-promoting because you're selling a product that will help them." —Carolyn Faye Kramer, actor/Actor's Fast Track coach

DEFINE YOUR BUYERS—
Who Needs Your Brand and
How do you plan to connect with them?

QUICK TIPS FROM VALORIE

- Ask yourself, "Who are your targeted buyers?"
- Who are ten people who cast the roles you've already identified as your brand?
- List your ideal project and all the details you know about it.
- Gather names of everyone you want to notice you. Make a list of them.
- Who are the writers on shows where you'd like to be booked?
- Make a list of your ideal project and all the details you know about it.
- Make a list of everyone you want to notice you.
- Who are the directors on shows where you'd like to be booked?

CHAPTER 4

BE A CONSTANT SELLER

At Actor's Fast Track, we help actors discover what they already have to sell *right now* and how to immediately utilize it to get work—with proven results.

When actors consistently follow an Actor's Fast Track sales plan that has been individually designed for them, they get work. How? They relentlessly put themselves out there and constantly sell themselves to buyers.

Most actors will tell you they knew from a very young age they wanted to be actors. They say being an actor is in their blood. It's what drives them and gives them satisfaction. Whether their parents enrolled them in acting and dance classes and they thrived in these or they just saw a movie on television and thought to themselves, "I want to do that—I can do that," it's who they are. But the sad truth is, many would-be actors never realize their true calling. Why?

Because selling is where a lot of actors get stymied.

They haven't learned how to effectively take action and put themselves out there. I'm very clear about this because that is often a big stopping point for my clients. This may even be the place in this book where you look woefully at the page and say, "Well, I guess this is where I check out. I can't do that."

But the most important take-away I want you to learn from this book is that *you* are the number one sales person in your own company. Actor's Fast Track can help you discover what you're selling. But you make your own success by getting out there and selling yourself.

The point is, you must sell YOU if you want to succeed. If you don't believe in your product and advocate yourself, fast-tracking your career will be nearly impossible.

> *"If you have a product you believe in and you hone your craft, it's much easier to sell it to others."*
> —Courtney Bandeko, actor/Actors Fast Track client

A lot of the rules looming in front of you are just myths.

Here are a few you may have heard yourself:

- You're not supposed to do a drop-off.
- You're not supposed to come to someone's office.
- You can only do this if you have an agent.
- If you didn't go to a good acting school, forget it.
- You're too old.
- You're not in the unions.
- You'll never have a career.
- You're not supposed to call casting directors on the phone and pitch yourself.

Sound familiar? The longer you're in one of the bigger markets, the more this is all going to get piled on top of you. They're going to tell you all the things you can't do. It's all bad advice! The "cant's" don't exist because there isn't a rulebook.

> *"Whatever your preconceived idea is of what the rules are, break them as much as possible; that's what Valorie teaches. If it's not working, do something else. I didn't really break any rules. All I did was use what was right in front of me. Essentially that's all you have to do when you break the rules. All the resources are at your fingertips. Use them."* —Bryan Coffee, actor/Actor's Fast Track client

There's a common misconception among actors that if they get an agent, they don't have to do anything but sit by the phone and wait for their agent to do the work for them. And agents will actually tell you that is their job, not yours.

The real truth is, though, that a lot of actors, rather than taking responsibility for themselves, put their entire career in an agent's hands thinking the agent is going to guide them through the whole process. And the agent doesn't do anything for them.

Actors then just sit and complain about their agent for the whole year instead of selling their product. They say things like, *"My agent doesn't submit me,"* which is usually not true.

But are they actively pitching you? Probably not. You have to find an agent who knows the buyers. The sad fact is, many of them don't know any more buyers than you do. There's just not a lot they can do for you.

It's like when you first learned you had to have money in the bank to write a check. Remember when you were a kid you innocently thought, "Oh, I can just write a check for a million dollars." It's with this same naive attitude that actors say, "I'm going to get an agent," because they've been told that's how you get a career. Just "write that million-dollar check."

Be confident and sell yourself.

My client, Ana Maria Perez, fought me for an entire year about selling herself. She was stuck on wanting an agent first.

So she found an agent who did nothing for her. At that point, she came to my Gamechanger three-day event. And despite my telling her what to do to get out there, she wasn't taking my advice. She just couldn't get past the seller point.

Finally, in January 2016, she confided in me, *"Val, I'm going to do what you tell me to do. But I'm **so** scared."* I assured her, "It's okay."

Her first drop-off, she carried $30 worth of cupcakes to a casting director's office. No one was there. Lights out. Gone. She texted me, *"What do I do?"* I answered back, *"Well, you have two choices: You can eat $30 worth of cupcakes or you can go to the next person on your list."*

She went to the next person on her list. To date she's had four auditions for major pilots and callbacks from that second person on her list. She pushed through her fear and crossed over that seller boundary.

"Eight seconds of courage can get you a lifetime of happiness." That is my favorite quote from my friend and coach Melissa McFarlane.

Sell to your true buyers.

So many people get caught up at the selling mark. Very few sail through that hurdle with flying colors. I've worked with thousands of actors and I can honestly say that those who have made it by simply getting an agent are about one percent, maybe two percent, of all working actors.

Agents don't pay you to act; casting directors do. Unions don't hire you; producers do. An agent is a seller. So is a union. And so are *you*. I can't emphasize this enough. **You are your own best seller!**

> "I got an acting career in L.A. because of Valorie. Initially, I hired her to get help with a presentation, thinking by getting an agent and a manager I would be set. But I learned it's not just about finding an agent. I had to sell myself. Being an actor is a business and I am in charge of it. I could have probably learned this over time on my own, but it would have taken me years rather than months. Valorie's experience is very extensive. And she's a business woman. Before I worked with her, I felt like I was just waiting to get in the game and I didn't know how. She's taught me how to get in the game." —Ana Maria Perez, actor/Actor's Fast Track client

As an actor who has clearly defined your own brand, you are the very best seller to represent yourself to hiring producers and casting directors because you are completely invested in selling your unique, specialized brand. And you are the only brand you are selling.

Even more perplexing is why you would wait until you find an agent who might potentially someday get your product out there when you can do it yourself now.

This makes no sense at all.

The key to active selling is to keep putting yourself out there.

Here's the thing: People sell everything all day long. My phone rings one hundred million times a day, and it's always someone either trying to give me money for my business or someone who wants to fix my house. Some days I answer the phone and the person who wants to fix my house calls me at the same time I'm looking for someone to fix my house. And the fact is, if the person calling to fix my house does other creative things to capture my attention, they will probably get my business a lot faster.

The primary reason you make a sales call is to get an audition. These tips will help you when making that contact.

- Ask for the person you are calling. Act like they should know you.
- Call to pitch for a specific role, invitation to a showcase or play.
- Get the name of the person you are talking to.
- Have a general pitch ready—For example, "Hey, it's Valorie Hubbard. I would like to pitch myself for (a particular role) and my recent credits include____."

I've been an actor for 31 years and I've heard people say, *"Oh, that's against protocol"* or *"Oh, you're not supposed to do that."* It's as though there's an unspoken rule book out there. But I've asked everyone. And there is no rulebook.

I'm not asking you to break the law. I'm just asking you to look beyond what is given to you. Take a moment and ask yourself, *"Is what they're telling me I can't do always true?"*

My rulebook is as follows:

- Don't make a quick decision.
- Always look at everything closely.
- Know what you're selling.
- Have a criteria list, which is a list of reasons you take a project.
- It's the Wild West out there, so keep a close eye on your money. There are a lot of people out there double-dipping right now, agents who take more commission from you than they're due.

"Valorie has always been a rule breaker and she encourages us to do the same."—Carolyn Faye Kramer, actor/Actor's Fast Track Coach

When and how to make sales calls.

- ALWAYS MAKE SALES CALLS! I know when you do this there will always be people telling you what you can't do. They'll say you can't pick up the phone and pitch yourself. But I'm here to tell you yes, you can.

- All of my clients have the same assignment. They must make at least five sales contacts each week—direct phone calls, drop offs, warm letters, or networking events.

- There are people who call casting directors every day. They're obnoxious and waste the casting director's time—and their own. But I know that's not you. You're going to be selective and only make that call when it counts, when you know there's a role for which you're perfect.

- If you can pitch yourself for two seconds on the phone and be very clear and to-the-point about why you are right for a role, you should **definitely** make that phone call.

That's breaking the rules. So there might be someone that tells you, *"Actors shouldn't call or drop by."* Okay, thanks, but no thanks. That's your opinion. It's not a rule. This is where breaking the rules comes in. Don't be afraid of being obnoxious if you make a cold call. Unless acting obnoxious is who you are, in which case you're going to need to fix that before going into the room, it's okay to start the sales conversation. You're not going to be obnoxious simply by sharing who you are.

My client Bryan Coffee is comfortable breaking the rules. But he didn't always feel this way.

> Bryan says, *"Before I started working with Valorie, I was not necessarily scared but I was hesitant to step out of what was "acceptable." I sat at home waiting for the agent's phone call. When I got a call, I'd go in and do a fantastic job.*

"I was definitely sending thank you letters and keeping in contact with the people I've met. But I wasn't actively pursuing new contacts. After working with Valorie, if I came across a part, I would think, 'Oh, I should be auditioning for that part—why am I not going in?'

Now I have my manager. We have a very good relationship! Or I will personally track down somebody to contact in either a casting office or production office and find out how I can get myself into that room. Basically, I'm way more active in my career and in trying to get what I specifically want. No more sitting back waiting for the phone to ring! That still happens, and that's great. But when there's an opportunity out there, I make sure I know how to get it."

Connect with buyers.

What I want to re-emphasize here is that selling requires connecting with the buyers (casting directors, producers, writers, directors, and ultimately the public). These are the people who are going to pay you. When you establish relationships with these people, you'll become a working actor. You have the RIGHT to go out and get the career you want. Stay on your course!

Show up as a viable product, ready to book.

Scott Cargle, an Actor's Fast Track coach, is a non-union, working actor because he made multi-six figures as the spokesperson for Cash Call. He walked through agent Courtney Peldon's door at Aqua Talent, primed and ready to book every co-star role as a homeless guy, snarky business guy, mean realtor, and asshole principal on Disney. He can get ALL of these.

Courtney knew he was a saleable product, so she signed him on the dotted line. Regardless of what people may say about having to be in the union to get an agent, it's not always true.

Here's a secret: you only need one casting director who loves you.

If you want more proof of the power of selling, just look at someone like Andrew Bachelor.

This kid is brilliant! I was his teacher in his master's program. And he did his undergraduate work at Florida state, which is an amazing acting university. He could probably do Shakespeare; he's a great actor.

He became famous by creating his own online alias persona, King Bach. He branded himself as an irreverent, edgy, goofy guy. His alias became so popular that he got eleven million followers on social media. And he did that simply by posting three Vines a day about trying to get a girl's attention. They are hilarious!

Andrew Bachelor didn't need an agent to do this; he just did it. He didn't ask anyone's permission; he simply put himself out there and it's worked for him.

His immense Vine popularity caught the attention of advertisers, who in turn paid him huge money to access his audience and reach his followers.

As a matter of fact, his posts were so entertaining, they ultimately garnered him a professional career. He used this highly unique self-created product to generate attention and eventually caught the notice of casting directors. He's now on two new TV shows.

If there's a role you know you are right for, it's okay to "break the rules" and bypass traditional methods for getting work. It worked for Andrew Bachelor. It can work for you too.

Stay confident.

Just go in and say, "This is what I do." Utilize relationship-building any way possible. And do it well. Consistently get in front of your buyers—the right people. And eventually you'll find your right fit.

BE A CONSTANT SELLER—
How do you plan to sell to your buyers?

VALORIE'S LAST MINUTE THOUGHTS:

- What is your viable product?
- Identify the main people you want to contact on your ideal project and how you plan to reach them.
- Can you think of times in your career when you could have "broken the rules" and didn't? How might the outcome have been different if you had?
- List five people (directors, casting directors, producers or writers) who have parts that are perfect for you. How do you plan to connect with them?
- What frightens you most about contacting casting directors, directors, or writers? How can you get past this fear and make your five calls or drop-offs?

CHAPTER 5

PITCH YOURSELF TO BUYERS

You are selling yourself, so highlight all your benefit to buyers. Share the number of hits you get on your website. Know how many Twitter followers, Facebook friends and YouTube views you have. Share the number of people, especially well-known people, interested in you. This is business, and business is motivated by money. So any proof you have that you can draw in money should be your objective.

To actively sell to key buyers, KNOW YOUR NUMBERS. These are where to start, but there are a million ways to get in front of buyers:

- Do drop-offs. If you know there's a part for which you are right, personally drop off your headshots and resume at the casting office and put a Post-It on it with the name of the role and part you want. Introduce yourself when you drop your packet off.
- Make at least five pitches and personal sales calls to the buyers on your targeted list.
- Send postcards to let buyers know what you've been up to. These are not a direct ask but they are good marketing for your business.
- Do a self-taping audition of a role you want and send it to the casting director.
- Send bi-weekly emails to buyers to stay front-of-mind.
- Go to casting workshops and introduce yourself to buyers.
- Follow people on social media.

- Think about a book have you read recently that you feel has a part in it for which you'd be perfect. Find out if anyone is planning to make it into a movie. If so, contact the writer requesting you be considered for the part.

Is snail mail obsolete?

No. Don't overlook snail mail. Warm letters are a great way to pitch yourself for a part you know is right for you. I've had incredible things happen to me from letters. They are a very important tool and can be very helpful.

The fact is, email is so overloaded now that if you reach out directly via snail mail, you may get great results. I just had a girl sign with a very big agency that told her, *"We called you in because we hadn't had a packet and letter like this in over a year."*

Or if they're making your favorite book into a movie, you could write to the author of the book and tell him, *"Listen, I've always felt akin to this part and I just want to pitch myself to you."* Incredible things can happen through writing something as simple as a letter.

Warm letters put you in front of buyers, break the *stranger barrier*, whisper in their ear and let you choose the message you want them to hear.

SELF-TAPE AND CREATE VIDEO LETTERS

A lot of my clients are also self-taping video letters. One of my clients, Bryan Coffee, who is the Metro PCS and on *Kevin from Work* and *Life in Pieces* has a video letter that is hilarious. He says, *"Hi. We don't know each other. I'm Bryan Coffee."* And then he'll do a clip of himself in the show. And he is HI-LARIOUS!

Bryan illustrates here how he uses video to promote himself.

> *"When I first signed up with Valorie, I contacted a video service because I was looking for an easy way to send my contact information to casting directors and say, "You're casting a part that's me." I talked with the guy in charge and we put together a Speed-Meet video letter of me talking to the camera in a general way. I introduce myself and let prospective buyers know what's*

going on with me. If it's more geared toward a specific casting director or producer, I address them directly.

"Along with that video of me just being me, I send a resume and my headshot to casting directors. It's basically like emailing a one-page website and it's been an effective selling tool for me, most definitely.

"Unfortunately, though it's not true for everyone, the major difficulty I'm finding is it's hard to get casting directors' emails. So it's not the perfect solution. But I've used it a couple of times and I think it's definitely helped. It's a good thing because it's an out-of-the-blue sales call to somebody I want to meet. Of the first three emails I sent out, I got an audition from one of the casting directors I'd never seen before."

USE SOCIAL MEDIA

Social media can be a very effective way to connect with buyers. I have a client who's fluent in ASL (American Sign Language) and she wanted to be on the show *Switched at Birth*. So she did a video of herself signing and found Dee Dee Bradley, the casting director, on Facebook. She sent Dee Dee a video of herself signing and got called in for an audition. She booked the part, which included a scene with Oscar-winner Marlee Matlin.

I have another client who found a casting director through social media and discovered the casting director had a blog. She went to the blog, started reading it, and got so inspired by it, she followed it. Then, in the way people often do through social media, they became friends.

A lot of casting decisions are also being made based on social media following. Case in point, I had a direct connection for one of my Actor's Fast Track coaches, Carolyn Faye Kramer, to a casting director who was casting a project in Canada that Carolyn was exactly right for. The part called for an actor that knew karate and Carolyn has a black belt! So I told Carolyn, "Pick up the phone and call her."

Carolyn did call but learned they were looking for an actor with 250,000 minimum Twitter followers. Casting directors want to make sure you're bringing followers along, people are going to watch the show, because that's what matters now.

Carolyn is now realizing the importance of reaching out with social media. *"Social media is the bane of my life because I haven't found the fun in it. Right now I don't really like it,"* she relates. *"But I know it's necessary for my career success."*

DO DROP OFFS.

As for the effectiveness of drop-offs, Carolyn is someone I got off the subject of agents very quickly. She took to going after the buyers right off the bat and what happened? In the first year of working with me, she booked eight commercials, two shows on ABC, and a big film before she ever got an agent, and then they dropped her.

She didn't come to the playground empty-handed. She just didn't know how to use it. But I got her right into the buyers and Bernie Telsey, who is the biggest casting director in New York City. He casts commercials, television, film and theater. All the best for everything.

One week she did three drop-offs for three different things to three different casting directors at the same office. But it was the same person at the front desk. She said, "I can't do this again!" And I said, "Yes, you can." And that's the office that got her everything. Two casting directors took a liking to her.

> *"I met Valorie at the perfect moment. I was so tired of running into the same wall over and over again. I'd turned my dream of being an actor down a notch to something that I thought would be more attainable. I was even going to quit my career. It's as though I was in a hole and Valorie came along and looked over the edge, reached down, and said, "Here, let me give you another way." So, I committed to working with her—and she helped me unearth my dream."* —Carolyn Faye Kramer, actor/Actor's Fast Track coach

BE AUTHENTIC.

Above all, I recommend with all communications that you are authentic and come from a place of confidence in your product. These people are business connections. Nothing scary. They are people doing a job, just like you. That's all. And they will eventually buy your product: YOU.

> *"I started training early in my life and I have confidence in what I can do. So when I go to a drop-off, I feel very confident. I've had a lot of people say, "What do you say to the casting directors?" Casting directors are just human beings doing a job and that job is finding actors. I'm an actor. I know I'm not going to be in everything they cast. But if I start that relationship and maintain it, even if it's a decade from now, because we've stayed in touch and I've kept growing and working the relationship, it'll align when they need my type. They'll go, "Oh, great! This one is perfect for Brian."* —Brian Majestic, actor/Actor's Fast Track client

One of my clients at Actor's Fast Track, Sara Banerjee, is fabulous at selling herself. She understands her niche and marketability and presents it to buyers in a genuine but direct way. Her authenticity garners her big results with legitimate studio and network roles.

Sara's auditioned for two series regulars on CBS, playing a lawyer and a doctor. She also got call backs for *ABC Showcase* and, just recently, for *Diversity Showcase 2016*. She did it all without an agent, a manager, series credit or series regular on her resume. **Not one!** She just did the leg work and stayed on track with the casting directors. She got called back in because she took the initiative and had a specific package that was marketable.

How did she do it?

Step One: *Sara discovered the first essential step to selling comes from understanding what you're selling—who you are and what your niche is.*

Step Two: *After developing her niche, Sara wrote a stand-out FedEx cover letter, including in it the roles for which she's best suited and what she'd studied. She highlighted her strengths as an actor. Actor's Fast Track helped her write it.*

Step Three: *She kept her eyes and ears open for parts that fit her essence and stayed keenly aware of what was out there. She paid close attention to current pilots.*

Step Four: *She relentlessly called casting directors if she found a pilot she was right for or a part that was distinctly "her." She would get called in.*

Step Five: *If she didn't get called in, she would make a follow-up phone call.*

Step Six: *She was fearless about taking that leap of faith and went for it. It worked!*

You must reach out to buyers directly. Don't be afraid, because nothing is ever out of reach.

SEND POSTCARDS AND MAIL-OUTS.

Twenty years ago, when I first met Rozie Bacchi, she was waiting tables at a restaurant that was a popular tourist attraction at the time. She didn't love the job, but it provided an income to pay rent and buy the tools that supported what we loved most: acting. Even then, Rozie knew instinctively acting was a business.

She was most likely my first coaching client. I helped steer her in the right direction and market herself as an actor. She understood right away that mail-outs were a way of connecting with industry folks. To this day, she celebrates her victories with them, both big and small, by sending mail outs. She never fails to make them laugh.

One day she mailed out a postcard just as an upcoming TV appearance happened to hit a casting director's desk. She booked a **huge** international commercial because her postcard got the buyer's attention. She was in the right place at the right time. But this didn't just "happen by luck." Rozie had been consistently marketing herself and doing regular outreach to her list; and her due diligence paid off.

Speaking of agents, when Rozie arrived at that audition, the casting director said, "I'm not sure why you weren't submitted for this role because you're perfect for it." The casting director, on seeing Rozie's postcard, requested her because her agent had not submitted her for the work. The part was for a 1960s mom from Brooklyn. She was perfect for the role.

She showed up, branded to the nines in a 1960s, cute little suit and bouffant hairstyle, nailed one line and was booked on the spot.

The point made here is not meant to disparage agents. Sometimes agents and managers through no fault of their own can just miss an opportunity for you. This is precisely why it is so important to be your own advocate, know what's going on, and take responsibility for your own career.

> As Rozie so aptly says, *"If opportunities aren't presenting themselves to you, then create your own. When I moved to Los Angeles, I just assumed because I had some good TV and film credits from New York that I would get work more easily. Hah! Little did I know that everyone in Los Angeles seemed to be involved in the "business" in one way or another. So I created an opportunity for myself—a solo show. As a result of my hard work on this, I was fortunate to get invited to perform at some of the biggest comedy theaters around town. This brought me work on late night TV shows because I promoted the shit out of myself!"*

DRESS THE PART.

My client Brian Majestic came into the business knowing exactly what he wanted and where he wanted to perform it. He had served in the military and knew he was a military guy. Once he realized he wanted to do television, he said, *"I'm going to be the police officer; I'm going to be the detective."*

You don't necessarily have to go out and get a police officer's uniform to do this, but you do have to go out there and see what's in use. So if you see yourself on TV, find out what they're wearing.

As for me, I get hired all the time because of what I wear. When I went to my *Agents of S.H.I.E.L.D.* audition, I wasn't given a script. I had to sign a disclosure agreement. It was all very secret and hush-hush. I'd never done the show but I watched it and thought to myself, "Oh, they wear rich lavenders and grays a lot."

So I simply found something in my closet that was periwinkle. And

I knew the audition part was going to be at a wedding, so I dressed up. I went in, looked at the line, and did it. Because I showed them that I belonged on the show, I got hired. For the part, they ended up dressing me in a beautiful periwinkle dress from Nordstrom.

When you are certain you belong on a show, just go out and claim your role.

Sometimes knowing which roles are right for you can bring surprising opportunities you might never have imagined on your own. In early May of this year I auditioned again for a film being cast by Emily Schweber. A casting director, she's cast me in five projects. One of them is the most fun project I've had since I've been in L.A.: a video game that was all motion capture (mocap). It was perfect for me and a BLAST!

It was more like doing Shakespearean theatre than any of the physical theatre I did for so many years in New York. Plus, my director, Tom Keegan, is famous for video games and mocap. Plus, when I walked into my audition, it was magical because Tom already knew what kind of actor I was and he hired me right away.

Performing for the video games was like doing theatre. It was **awesome!** OH, MY GOD! It was **SO** much fun. I'm doing things like killing. At one point, I stick a crowbar through a zombie's head! But, I mean, the emotion of everything is real. I get my arm blown off. I replace it with a laser gun. I fix an airplane. I see my husband, who I thought was dead and eaten by zombies, and we have a reuniting. It's EPIC, epic acting!

How much more fun is it to act in the projects you were born to do? The good news is, ***it's completely within your reach to do so.***

Once you know the shows you are right for because you've said who you are and know what you do better than everyone else, then you need to go and find the people who are involved in these shows and sell to them.

You must push into life and go toward it. You can turn people off by doing this but you can also turn people on. Because the people who can get behind what you're pushing will never see it unless you push it. Quit can't be in your blood.

Be consistent.

If you're always putting out content, you're going to get people's attention. That's why using the same picture over and over again is important because people will eventually say, "Oh, wait! I know this girl." They don't know how they know you but they've seen your picture a million times so they think they do.

My client Brian Majestic is incredibly organized and consistent in his outreach to casting directors. He bases his outreach on what he's learned through Actor's Fast Track. Here's how he got started:

- He did drop-offs because he couldn't afford workshops.
- He made a notebook entitled, "The Brian Majestic Agency" because he had no representation.
- He started looking through the breakdowns and what was casting to get a feel for what people were doing.
- Then he dropped off his headshot and resume.
- He sent postcards with his headshot and agent's information.
- He attended workshops and after the workshops, sent follow-up thank you cards.
- In 8-10 weeks, he sent another postcard—and in 3 months, another one.
- In 6 months, he sent a follow-up letter sharing what he'd been doing in his career and attached his business card, headshot, and agent's number in the letter.
- In 8 months, he did a drop-off just to reconnect.
- He made a huge spreadsheet of who I'd be contacting for the next three months.

By doing this, he managed to get a 15-minute conversation with a casting director who ended up casting him in Criminal Minds three weeks later. Now he stays regularly in touch with at least 35 casting directors who know who he is.

Brian is doing it right. If your face and interaction with others is out there enough, people will begin to think they know you. This can also be done through letters, postcards, social media, a YouTube channel or by sending out emails. And it's even better if they have met and talked with you. It all comes down to consistency.

Know your marketplace and competition.

Keep an active list of your target markets. Who exactly are you selling to and what are their likes, dislikes and preferences?

Know your competitors and any current trends going on with buyers. What are the roles that are getting booked? And, because buyers of actor's work are subject to public trends and preferences, also watch what the public is buying. This should include your most current knowledge of the marketplace, and don't guess! Be accurate. You can use this information when you sell yourself to buyers.

Use your money wisely to build sales opportunities.

To build your career as an actor, you need to invest in yourself, which is a weird thing to consider because in this society, particularly as a woman, we're not always encouraged to invest in ourselves. However, as with any sole proprietorship, if you want to start a business, you need to be ready to invest in it so it can grow.

This is no less true of your acting career. Be ready to spend money on activities that will expand your circle of influence—casting workshops, conferences, seminars, film festivals, gifts, and workshops. These are networking opportunities that will grow your career.

Don't scrimp on growth opportunities because they can, and often do, increase your connections and visibility. Once you see the wisdom of spending money to make money, you'll want to invest capital in your business.

Network, network, network.

Effective networking is also a big part of constant selling.

Most of the networking events I've found designed for actors just turn out to be a bunch of actors standing around talking to a bunch of actors, *and that's what people think networking is*. They're wrong. These types of events are not going to get you anywhere.

For example, I was on the roof of The Standard Hotel in Hollywood and there was a group of actresses sitting around a fire pit looking beautiful. They were all friends. I went up to them and asked," *Hey, girls. How are you? So who's your favorite director*?" They looked at me as though I had three heads. I just wanted to stop right there and say, "Listen, go home. Pack your bags. Because you will never work as an actress." Why? Because I'm older. I could be the head of casting for CBS. So you want to be informed in case that happens. DON'T BE STUPID!

What is an appropriate and beneficial networking event for actors? How do you get in front of buyers?

You can start by doing one or more of the following:

- Attend film festivals.
- Participate in casting workshops.
- Attend acting classes.
- Go to film screenings.
- Frequent performances.

Why attend film festivals?

- First, a film festival is a GREAT networking event because there are a lot of filmmakers there. They're the buyers. And though the concentration at a film festival is directing, writing, and hardly ever acting, you can make great connections there.

- Frequently I also find when you buy a weekend pass to a film festival, they also have numerous panels. There will be a lot of casting directors there, too. And there are parties. Go to the parties! Amazing opportunities can spring into your life when you least expect it.

» For example, I was at The Women's Film Festival in Beverly Hills, California. They had a panel with every major casting director in the business and it was in **a lounge setting!** And I was the only actor there and I had my manager with me. I felt like I was a kid in a candy store and I was the only kid allowed in it.

» Another time, I was at an opening night at the Tall Grass Festival in Wichita, Kansas, and my film was in it. Ronnie Yeskel, whom I know and who was casting director for *Pulp Fiction*, was at the party! They flew her in because they were doing a retrospective on *Pulp Fiction*. This was a direct connection, right there. And no one else in Wichita, Kansas was going to be talking to Ronnie Yeskel like I could be talking to her.

What film festivals are worth attending?

- *Without a Box* is a website that lists every film festival. Filmmakers submit their films here to be considered for film festivals. *South by Southwest* in Austin, Texas; *Sundance* in Park City, Utah; *Seattle Film Festival* in Seattle, Washington; and film festivals in Toronto and Palm Springs. These can put you in rooms with a lot of important people who can move your career forward.

Once you're in front of your buyers, here are ways to ensure they remember you:

- **Know your brand and bring your literature.** By literature, I mean your marketing packet: your headshot, resume, business card, postcards and other mail-outs. Know what you want to experience. Having a clear intention or objective is always important when you enter a scene. What are you doing there and what do you want? **Get really clear.** Knowledge is power and the more you know walking into any event, the better.

- **Have your tag or pitch line ready and be aware of who you want to meet.** Likely, it will be someone you didn't expect to, so be ready. If you're putting yourself out there, someone you meet will change your life.

- **Focus on the person in front of you.**

Any acting class teaches you the most important person in a scene, acting wise, is the other person. The same is true with networking. You need to be focused on the person you're talking to and picking up whatever interest they may have and whatever they do. Show genuine interest in who they are, and know that they're in front of you for a reason. Finish that conversation and then move on to the next.

- **Be topical and current in your conversation.** It's important at film festivals and other networking events to have a few topics you're ready to talk about other than acting. Know what people are discussing in the news and social media. It's also important to know what people are talking about to learn what matters to them. Find who they are, what interests they have and share that part of yourself with them.

- Women and politics are big topics of conversation right now, as are women in film. Talking about films is a great ice-breaker and an easy way to make connections. If you're going to a film festival, be sure to see the films. People will be talking about what the newest hot film is at the festival and you'll want to be informed.

- Talk about your craft or a current project you're working on. By doing so, you can position yourself in the marketplace. I've served on many panels, boards, and nominating committees, so I've seen every famous actor talk on a panel. The one thing I've observed is they all have a great, religious appreciation for their craft. I saw *Gravity* three times. I love that movie. When I saw Sandra Bullock talk, I was amazed by her. She was in the craft conversation!

> *"I have my biggest success networking at film festivals where I can meet people and allow my personality to come out. Relaxing and just being myself socially has given me the maximum amount of connections. It's ironic that the thing I was most afraid of—approaching casting directors directly—is the very thing I would make my home in."* —Mary Somers, actor/Actor's Fast Track client

Attend casting workshops.

- When you come into the acting workshop, the casting director answers questions and then assigns seats to everyone. You get 15 minutes to get up and do your scenes. Sometimes you go in by yourself and bring a prepared monologue or prepared scene from TV for the casting director. Other times they are group modalities.

Why are casting workshops good for actors?

- At a cost of $35-$100, these are a pay-to-play situation but can be a very good investment for actors because casting directors attend. You do scenes with them, they work with you and get to know you as an actor. You can demonstrate your product there in person.

How can casting workshops get you hired?

- In a casting office, the casting director's name will be on the door, followed by the associates' names, which means they are also functionally running the casting offices. Sometimes associates branch off and form their own casting offices and hire assistants. So a lot of times, the people who go to these casting workshops are their assistants.

Why are casting workshops important to casting directors?

- In this fast-paced world, casting workshops are a big support to casting offices, and, therefore, potentially beneficial to actors. Let's say you're a big office and you're casting a show that has 20 one-liner co-stars. You've made a relationship with someone in a casting workshop whom you think is a good actor. You can quickly bring this actor in and book a co-star. It saves offices a lot of time and energy.

Currently the future of casting workshops in Los Angeles is uncertain. But it's my best hope they will continue because they're good for the industry and great for actors.

"I make connections with casting directors by going to casting workshops because I know I'll stand out in the room due to being prepared. When I go into a room or do a drop-off, I know I'm bringing my authentic self. Valorie talks about "connect; don't impress." But when it's time to do the work, I bring forth the parts of myself I want seen, whatever character I'm playing, but also Carolyn Faye Kramer, the actor." —Carolyn Faye Kramer, actor/Actor's Fast Track coach

Another simple but powerful way to connect with buyers is by giving small gifts.

- My agent told me when he opened in L.A. eight or nine years ago, he spent $3,000 on gifts to send to all the casting directors because he knew he had to stake his place as someone who was reputable. He's a smart businessman and that's why he's a good agent.

"Before I worked with Valorie, sending gifts seemed really hokey and cheesy to me. I felt like I was trying to get something from them. But now it doesn't. I had to rewire my thinking to say, "No, I don't really want anything from them. All I want is to create that relationship and that friendship." And what is wrong with that? There's really nothing wrong with that. That's my relationship with all my agents; I'm absolutely genuine with them." —Bryan Coffee, actor/Actor's Fast Track client

Take classes—you can sell in them.

- For example, if I want to do comedy, a good route for me as an actor is to go take a class at the Upright Citizens Brigade (UCB), Groundlings, or Second City because these places are frequented by the people I want as my buyers.

WHEN AND HOW TO GET A GOOD AGENT

As I mentioned earlier, you don't need an agent to get started. Start at the top and sell yourself directly to buyers. **Then**, once you get good at selling what you offer, you can hire other people to sell for you. But you may have to school them in how to sell you. There are some "really good eggs" out there. I have an amazing agent. But there will also be others that have a different viewpoint about how to sell you. Their approach won't be based on the principles in this book. They will need guidance.

If you've been actively paying attention to my advice in chapters two and three of this book, you've probably already booked a few jobs because you've learned how to capture the attention of buyers and book work. Now you can use these jobs as leverage to get a decent agent who is going to genuinely assist you with getting into rooms. Ultimately, your agent becomes your business partner, not just someone who has your information in a file.

How to Prepare for Meeting With an Agent

When looking for a good, effective agent, I follow the advice of author Brian O'Neill. In his book, *Acting as a Business*, O'Neill says you need to always be ready to answer the following questions before going into any room:

- Tell me about yourself. Why are you an actor? What inspires you? What story is uniquely your own?
- How do you see yourself? In other words, what roles are perfect for your brand and why?
- Where do you see yourself professionally in five years? Where do you want to take your career?
- Who do you know in the business who the agent may also recognize favorably? Does that person know your work?

I always have answers to these questions prepared before walking into any office.

Also, be ready to tell a story about yourself that brings your personality into the room. It could be something from your acting career or personal life. I like to tell the story of how I began my acting career when I dramatically threw myself down the stairs at three years old. It's a fun, engaging way to bring myself immediately into the room.

Then you need to be able to talk vibrantly about your product. Learn from the way some politicians talk subtly about themselves to make the recent roles you've played an undercurrent of what you truly want to communicate about yourself and who you know.

For example, if you just had a role in *Workaholics*, you know the casting director of that show, Alyssa Weisberg. You won't have to out-and-out say you know Allyssa Weisberg. But it will be understood by the agent. Then you can talk about immediately about the kind of character you played because you've already identified how you see yourself and who you know.

How to Know an Agent Is the Best One for You

If I'm an agent and I'm looking for a client, and you walk into the room prepared, you're coming into the room as an equal partner. As an equal, you can then look confidently across the desk and ask yourself, *"Can this person get me into the rooms that I need to get into?"*

- For example, if I walk into a room with an agent and I know that I'm selling myself for Disney and ABC and ABC Family, and his major clients are in Broadway shows and only on CBS shows, I think, *"Uh, okay. That's not a good office for me."*

You must be smart about your brand and be certain you find the right agent to be the best partner for your business. As an actor who has clearly defined your own brand, you are the very best seller to represent yourself to hiring producers and casting directors because you are completely invested in selling your unique, specialized brand. And you are the only brand you are selling.

Be responsible, brave, and advocate yourself. An agent is there to assist you but doesn't do it for you. It's up to you to interview agents to find the one that will support you best.

How to Effectively Work With Agents and Managers

Theoretically, the difference between agents and managers in "storybook land," is that managers are supposed to guide the trajectory of your career, so they are not just pointing and clicking, which is how agents submit you for projects. But it's never really like this.

So when I meet with managers, I am thinking more about being myself. I'm owning my own brand and career's trajectory, which is how I end up booking what's right for me. In that spirit, I once had an agent tell me, *"You don't need a manager; you're your own manager."* Which is quite true.

Agents are the people who are supposed to be franchised to the union, which means they can negotiate a contract for you if are a union member. And a good agent can mean that the casting directors answer the phone when your agent calls.

Agents and managers can double submit you for the same role and pitch you, as well. So they can either electronically pitch or they can pick up the phone and verbally pitch. And then your agent, or if you're a higher-end actor, your attorney, negotiates the contract for you.

That's the difference between agents and managers. And it doesn't matter which comes first, the chicken or the egg.

When to get an Agent

This is not to say you shouldn't EVER hire an agent; just be patient and wait until you have booked your own work. Then, as an actor with a body of work in tow, you'll get a much better agent who will ultimately be very helpful to your career.

But be a shark at first!

In other words, if you're standing still, you're going to find an agent who is also standing still.

But if you're moving on your own like a shark that always moves forward to breathe, you're going to meet another shark that is also moving forward. This will be an agent who, just like you, is on the hunt, already swimming through deeper water. THAT'S a good agent.

Find people who are going to understand how to sell you; then put them on your team.

Because I'm challenging the protocol of the agent-actor business relationship, if you come through the Actor's Fast Track system, sometimes you're going to run into trouble getting an agent or a manager due to the new mindset you'll develop. You'll play as an equal and some of them aren't used to that. But when you do get an agent that understands your determination and self-reliance and knows that you are standing strong in your career, you'll have someone on your team who can really get you the results you want.

> *"I initially hired Valorie to help me make a presentation, thinking by just getting an agent and a manager I would be set. But I learned it's not just about finding an agent. Being an actor is a business; I have to sell myself. I could have probably learned how to do this over time, but it would have taken me years rather than months. Now I have an agent and a manager. And they are more interested in getting me out there because they can see I am being proactive about my career."* —Anna Maria Perez, actor/Actor's Fast Track client

Principles of selling don't change over time.

By the time you read this book, the best method for selling yourself may have changed.

But the principle of selling won't change. The most important thing in selling will **always** be getting yourself out there to the people who are going to buy you.

Always remember that buyers are the people who need to get your focus, not sellers. The best course of action is just to start. Once you know what you're selling, then you'll know who to sell it to—and who to put at the top of your "Hit List."

> *"I need to fight for my own dream. Nobody's going to fight for it as strongly as I am because I'm the one who wants it the most."* —Ana Maria Perez, actor/Actor's Fast Track client

MARKETING AND SALES CONNECTS YOU
with your buyers. How do you plan to sell yourself?

VALORIE'S EXTRA THOUGHTS:

- What questions about yourself will you have ready? How will you answer them when you walk into an agent or manager's office?

- What engaging story will you use to bring your personality into the room? Write down some ideas.

- What five film festivals could you attend where you could meet casting directors who are working on projects you're interested in?

- What classes or workshops are associated with the route you want to go on as an actor? Identify these and sign up!

- What content do you plan to start putting out on social media immediately?

- What skills do you have that are unique to the roles you want?

BUSINESS MINDSET AND COMPETITIVE ADVANTAGE: HOW TO STAND OUT IN THE CROWD AND LEAP TO SUCCESS

CHAPTER 6

MINDSET DETERMINES YOUR SUCCESS OR FAILURE

What is mindset?

Mindset is your habitual thinking, your beliefs, how you view the world, the acting industry and yourself. It's your attitude about life, your worthiness, and your career because how you think about all these determines how you'll act and what you'll do.

> *"I had an acting teacher who said people often go into acting to get acknowledged, and I think that's true. I come from a family of four boys. Acting was a way for me to stand out and be acknowledged. But I know now that being an actor doesn't validate or define me as a human being. I do still love to be acknowledged. It's a wonderful thing for anyone, whatever your passion, career, or life. To be seen is very important. But I'm not in such a rush anymore to get acknowledged. I'm no longer trying to get rid of the neediness or wanting to get someone to love me."* —Brian Majestic, actor/Actor's Fast Track client

What is a business mindset?

Having a business mindset means you've combined your creativity as an artist with the savvy perspective and acuity of an entrepreneurial business person. The duality in this approach to acting is what separates successful actors from those struggling in the industry.

Strategic planning, constant action, and understanding your market and buyers are all aspects of developing a business mindset. This means, as I've mentioned before and re-emphasize here, that in addition to continuous development of your craft as actor, you have to think strategically in the same way any successful business person would.

> *"Break the mindset that society, industry, and our family have told us we have to follow to get an acting career. This is coming from people who just regurgitate what their teachers or family have told them. People who follow all these rules end up not getting the career they've dreamed of. The only good rule is the golden one. Just be a decent person.* —Brian Majestic, actor/Actor's Fast Track client

How to develop business mindset.

First and foremost, having a business mindset means that you think positively about yourself and your talent. A change of perspective means you know the value of what you can bring to your buyers rather than what you want or need from them. Think of yourself as providing an essential product they need for the success of **their** projects.

In other words, know with certainty that you are helping them solve their problem. It's a subtle shift of perspective but it makes a world of difference when you walk into a room to audition for a role. Rather than apologetically or desperately asking for a part, you're presenting casting directors with a golden opportunity to book just the right person for that role, the very actor they've been waiting for, YOU.

You've probably heard all kinds of stories that are counter to how to approach the business of acting. But don't let doubt or fear stand in your way. Find your courage and move forward.

Be confident and focused in your intention. Ignore the boundaries arbitrarily set by others. Be strong enough to stand in the belief that you're right for the role you desire. When you do this with conviction, you'll get hired.

Taking Action = Reduced Fear

You alone are in charge of your future. No one else is! So it is up to you to believe you are good enough to enter the marketplace. But you must be in the right mindset to realize your talent and potential.

> *"When I first started working with Valorie, I got nervous about my financial situation and told her I was in dire straits and thought I should back out. She said, "If it's all about money, I can let you go. But maybe it's something else. Maybe you're afraid of something." And as I analyzed it, I realized she was right. We get comfortable where we are even though we want to be somewhere else. Taking that leap is very scary because we know failure. And when you realize you can have what you want, it's kind of frightening because we're told that we can. But we're not really taught that we can."* —Brian Majestic, actor/Actor's Fast Track client

How does mindset affect your career as an actor?

If you believe the industry is too hard, you're not good enough, or you don't deserve to have an amazing acting career for whatever negative self-stories you've allowed yourself to believe, you'll have an extremely difficult time manifesting a great acting career. Your own mind may actually be sabotaging your best efforts. I've seen it happen! Feel the fear and do it anyway.

Occasionally, I still have clients whose mindset stops them from succeeding. In some cases, actors have the world available to them and are right within the reach of a great career but won't take the action to make it happen. Why won't they take the right actions to seize what is right in front of them? It's aggravating to me, and sad!

But if you feel as though you aren't worthy of success or believe you're always having crappy results, the problem is likely due to your mindset. Changing your perspective is almost always the solution.

> "Before I started working with Valorie, I was literally on my own, struggling to make ends meet. I've been in and out of L. A. for years doing all the right stuff. I just wasn't connecting with jobs. I was going to casting workshops, but I wasn't following up with anybody. I wasn't reaching out to people to get them to know me. I was documenting everything I did, but I wasn't ever going beyond it to contact them again. Valorie told me to contact them and I thought, "I can talk to these people? Oh, my gosh! I had glorified them and given them all my control. And it's not at all like that." —Esme Baneulos, actor/ Actor's Fast Track client

THE FORMULA

Here's a thought-provoking formula to keep in mind:

Crappy mindset + crappy behavior = crappy results.

> "When I changed my mindset, I realized it was scarier to stay at home and have things not happen than to leave my fear aside, push myself out there and make them happen. This can be a very tough business. Learn to be patient and courageous. Don't get discouraged." —Anna Maria Perez, actor/Actor's Fast Track client

Nearly 100 percent of the time we're held back by fear of taking an action that has nothing to do with how talented an actor you are. It's just fear that gets us stuck. You can't read the mind of a casting director. You just need to get out there, be completely present in the performance you're doing, ignore all that inner, critical self-talk and impress them!

My client Sara Banerjee says working with Actor's Fast Track has made her more confident in her craft.

> "I'm not such a Nervous Nellie. The more I work with Actor's Fast Track, the easier this becomes. You establish new patterns of thinking and mind shifts that organically just happen over time. And I don't think you realize how much you've changed until you look back. For me, it's been huge. You retrain your brain for better results, like training your muscles at the gym."
>
> "Do what the coaches tell you to do and slowly, you'll learn

to present yourself in a more positive, confident, self-supportive manner. Actor's Fast Track is very good at helping you wade through the fear to get to the other side. Establish the habit, establish the pattern. If you do that, the fear just starts diminishing by itself. You start talking yourself out of negative self-fear."

Using visualization techniques can help you shift your mindset.

Mindset shift is important because it keeps you grounded and calm, and helps you get out of your head. The visualization Sara Banerjee uses to get out of her head switches for whatever part she's going out for at the time. But she says her process is the same.

> "For ABC Showcase, I visualized opening an envelope from ABC and the letter inside said, "Congratulations, Sara Banerjee, on your entrance into ABC Showcase 2016." I visualized everything about this imaginary letter including its type font, and I went word for word."

A couple of seasons ago, Sara had to go out for a few season regulars. She had 12 hours to memorize five to seven pages of lines the night before the audition. She had three scenes to go through, and, because they wanted to see a range, a number of different characters. Sara related how she forged through her fearful mindset about the audition.

> "I told myself "the story" that I could not memorize those lines. And when you tell yourself, 'I have a terrible memory; I can't memorize lines,' you start believing it. Valorie sat me down at 11 o'clock at night, coached me through all this stuff and calmed me down. She was a champ! And I ended up doing fine. I would have missed some HUGE opportunities had Valorie not just told me to go for it. It's also important to realize that even if you don't get hired, being a part of an audition is valuable because it preps you to nail your role the next time."

There's a reason mindset isn't first in this book.

The fact is, actors don't connect with business mindset until they are comfortable with selling and putting themselves out there. Due to the very nature of our craft, actors tend to be emotional. But this doesn't serve you when you're conducting business.

When you're in a business mindset, you need to take your emotions out of your interactions. Don't take the no responses you get personally. It's not about you. It depends only on what the casting director envisions for a role in a specific project.

Your product might not be what they need for a killer recipe, but that's okay because there are other recipes. It's not about you as a person. You must be able to keep a balance between caring enough to give your best performance and valuing being in the audition. Your goal becomes not just to get the job, but to book the room so casting directors will bring you in again. Feel good about what you did, regardless of the outcome.

Don't focus on what other people are doing or let it affect you. Brush yourself off and keep going. Know that it's a success to get in the room for an audition. If you don't book the role you want, move on to the next audition. The part that's right for you is out there, waiting for you to connect with it.

> *"Get out of your own way. It's not about having the best agent, the best demo reel, the best resume. If you know what your marketability is and you put yourself out there, you will work. I've gone out for really big stuff, season regulars, without a reel. Take action persistently and keep going. You just have to be present and stop caring so much about what other people think. Just go forward and do it. If you're getting out there, someone, somewhere, some way is going to hire you for something. If you persevere and don't have fear, someone is going to hire your ass. I promise you!"* —Sara Banerjee, actor/Actor's Fast Track client

Live at Choice founder Belanie Dishong works with Actor's Fast Track clients and has tapped into what's stopping them from moving into business mindset. She helps actors identify, hone, and change their mindset.

She says they're getting dressed up to do drop-offs and four hours later, they're still sitting on Facebook or the couch having never gone out. And they then give the excuse they can't go out because it's rush hour. Fear of actively selling themselves is getting in their way.

> *"Actors have a common thread. They feel through their acting they have something to tell the world—and through their art and voice in acting, they want to give something significant and meaningful to the world. Even before they get work, they often feel that through their voice they've finally found a way to express themselves. And yet the very thing that they felt held them back is part of the negative self-belief that is holding them back."* —Belanie Dishong, Live at Choice

Mindset for anyone, including actors, is the deciding factor for how you're going to live.

Mindset can create fabulous results when the actor's mind is being supportive. But you can take that very same person, and even though they know in their mind they're incredible and can visualize being a fabulous actor, they freeze. Limiting, critical mind-chatter debilitates them and stops them from taking an action. Often the best actors are the ones who are just watching movies at home because they can never move off the couch, take it to their dream and become a full-time, working actor.

> *"I never thought about just walking into someone's office, ever. For me, the biggest mindset shift I've had through working with Valorie is that I'm also a professional and I can walk into a casting office and show them my product. My big challenge is in being brave about doing this kind of outreach and getting behind what I believe in and am selling."* —Courtney Bandeko, actor/Actor's Fast Track client

What we can't see *can* hurt us.

We all have a survival mechanism inside our minds. And we hear our mindset-chatter through this filter. For example, many actors believe that standing up and speaking, getting on the stage, and going to an interview frightens everybody. So there's a common misbelief in the acting world that this fear is something actors just have to learn to endure.

The root of this belief, however, is often something actors can't see in themselves. And that is their mindset that nobody is going to want them. The hardest struggle actors have is just taking action because what governs their belief system is often so contrary to what it has to be in order to take action. Their belief system is going to determine whether or not they have the ability to go after business.

Success is belief driven.

Taking no action or being highly successful is all belief-driven. When actors have access to knowing what's behind their belief system, that negative, debilitating, limiting belief about themselves as being unsuccessful or struggling, whatever their belief system is, will just completely melt away and they'll be able to take the action.

> *"Valorie has taught me that I am valuable without already being a star, having a job, money or awards. I have something valuable to contribute."* —Courtney Bandeko actor/Actor's Fast Track client

Don't self-sabotage. Be a belief-basher-smasher!

My client Mary Somers knows how powerful the critical voices that linger behind our personal fear and doubt curtain can be. She says her mother once told her she was fat and it became a defining belief that affected her self-image and ability to get out there and sell herself. She explains how hard it's been to shift that mindset.

> *"It's interesting how something said to you by someone you care about can become a magnified voice in your mind, even if you only hear it once. Somehow it continues to be the negative story you tell yourself. My mother, who grew up in a Russian ballet community, told me I was fat. And yes, if you're comparing me to a Russian ballerina, I'm absolutely going to be bigger than her. Valorie helped me realize that I didn't have to **listen** to the negative stories I was telling myself about being "the fat girl." However, the impact of being told I was fat was huge, and something I struggle with to this day."*

It's our perception and the meaning we give to what happened that determine our mindset.

Belanie Dishong teaches that freedom in a person's mindset is not about being free of circumstances they think caused a belief. For example, Mary's mom may never have said Mary was fat. Mary may have only assumed that based on a misinterpreted glance, her own thoughts about Russian ballerinas being thin, or her mom simply asking, *"Isn't that dress a little too tight on you?"* When we look at the exact words that were said, it's never about what really happened.

People tend to believe that if they are free of a circumstance and it just goes away, they can then take action. The problem is, it's not possible to make a circumstance disappear. It's there. You can make new choices, get a new outcome and have a new set of circumstances, but you can't make the initial one go away. But your **perception** of it **can** go away.

When a person knows what's behind their belief system, what's hidden that's driving that belief, and sees and takes ownership of what they've made up about a circumstance, then all the beliefs that follow are resolved. The circumstances of what they thought was the issue no longer have any impact or value. This experiential process clears a path to set them free of negative self-chatter. They can step into their greatness and deliver on the results.

Mindset sets the stage for success or failure.

To be released from a belief that is blocking your way, you must connect with it and make the shift permanent. We've been taught that we must figure out our problem and then endure and work around it the rest of our lives. However, you can stop the chatter. It goes away when you reveal what's truly behind your belief system.

The successful actor is the one who said a long time ago as a child that that there was **nothing** that was going to stop them. Because in that part of who they said they were, they've empowered themselves and they deliver on it!

However, I may talk with this same group of actors and some are suffering repeated relationship breakups and others are putting their profits up their nose because they aren't free of those other self-debilitating things they've said they're not. They have a big vision and they know, no matter what, they can deliver on that vision. But they stop short at "the sell" because they're shut down in their negative self-belief. They write their own scripts about why they're stuck and why they're not getting hired.

You can have the best strategy in the entire world, but if your mindset is something other than a belief system that is aligned with a successful outcome, you'll never do it. It will go anywhere from *"I can't get off the sofa to take action"* to oversleeping through one of the biggest interviews you could have ever had. Sabotage is that fast!

> *"What's behind the belief system determines the belief system, and the belief system is changeable. Mindset is what is making the difference for Valorie and her clients."*—Belanie Dishong, Live at Choice

Change your perception = Change your results

The biggest mistake actors make is spending time sitting around on Facebook waiting for the phone to ring. The phone isn't going to ring just because you feel good about yourself. You're going to have to stretch yourself to your most uncomfortable spot and get out there.

My client Esme Banuelos has faced a lot of mindset challenges head-on. She's a great example of an actor whose determination to succeed has superseded all her obstacles. Nothing is going to stop her from realizing her dream. Despite distance, she's making considerable progress.

> "It was scary for me to hire Valorie because I live in the middle of frickin' Kansas! I don't live in California, Chicago, or New York where everything is happening. And I don't have an agent or a manager. My hardest mindset to overcome has been, 'How do I make a career from the middle of nowhere?'

"When I was at Valorie's three-day Game Change, she asked everyone what five steps they were doing that week to get the attention of buyers. I kept thinking, "I can't do that. I'm from Kansas." Then literally, the light bulb turned on. 'Wait a minute! I'm not in Kansas right now. What am I complaining about? I'm literally in California!'

"Immediately the next day, I bought a bunch of gift bags with candy, put my headshot with them, and ran around town doing drop-offs. One of those drop-offs was to Hulu, which is what got me an audition with them."

Stop tolerating situations that stand in the way of your success.

Most of the time what actors think of themselves keeps them from taking action and realizing their dreams. However, occasionally it is a toleration.

What is a toleration? A toleration is that pesky thing you're been meaning to do and just haven't quite come around to doing that is taking up space in your brain and distracting you from focusing on your career. You are tolerating it because you are in denial and have not or will not change the reality of the situation.

It's something you are putting up with and procrastinating on changing—the pile of dirty laundry in your bedroom, the broken light switch in your living room, etc. It could also be your boyfriend, girlfriend, wife, mother, father, or your spirituality. You get the drift.

Actors can also get derailed by tolerating their own self-doubt! This is a big distraction. Stop it!

> "Recreating mindset is a journey. When you combine mindset and strategy, you'll walk down a path to execute your strategy. Valorie is addressing actors' strategic change. As a coach of mindset, I'm addressing mindset. What happens is that you'll address one aspect of your mindset and feel great. But at some point, you'll cross into another circumstance in life that is not one you've stood in before. When it's activated, you'll get stuck for a different reason. Valorie is very innovative because she brings in the coaching that will help kick you those cans right out of your way." —Belanie Dishong, Live at Choice

Don't let a no response from a contact make you stop trying to reach out to them.

I have to do *15* touches to someone on my list to get their attention. If a part of these boomerang, I'm just going to keep sending out correspondence, correspondence, correspondence.

But what most actors think is, *"My correspondence! Oh, my god! They didn't answer me. They must not like me. What am I going to do?"*

Shut up! Stay confident—and just keep going. Correspondence, correspondence, correspondence, correspondence. If after a gazillion correspondences you've never had one response, then it's time to think about what's wrong with your correspondence.

> *"I took a big leap of faith in my life to put aside everything else that was distracting me to pursue my career. I've learned to focus on what's important in terms of getting where I want to be. I think a lot of creative people are distracted by all the shiny possibilities they could pursue. Valorie has helped me get really succinct and have the belief that these actions I'm taking are working."* —Carolyn Faye Kramer actor/Actor's Fast Track client

Don't let self-doubt get in the way of action

Sometimes an actor can have a great opportunity but due to a mindset of self-doubt, just not follow up on it. My client Carolyn Faye Kramer had an email address of a casting director from a family member who met someone at a wedding through another connection. She'd been holding off from connecting with this person even though she kept thinking it could be a good opportunity. She'd been hesitant to sell herself for a couple of months. I told her to reach out. We sat down and wrote an email together.

Carolyn still laughs talking about it. *"I remember hitting the "send" button and wanting to vomit after I sent it! But I immediately got a friendly response because it was just another human I was writing—and she was a lovely person."*

A few weeks later, Carolyn was called into the casting director's office for a commercial audition. Not only was she cast for that commercial, but she got eight more commercial shots. So right off the bat, simply from taking that first step, she got five days of shooting.

Talent can take you to a certain point, but you also have to push through your fear of reaching out to get hired. Ignore the signs that say, *"Actors, do not enter. Do not call."* You have to be the person who says, *"No, I will do that because all I'm doing is offering to solve their problem."*

> *"When I first got involved with Actor's Fast Track, my background was mostly in theatre work. But I had started contacting casting directors with the intention of getting into television. Valorie told me, "Carolyn, you're going to get two television shows this year." I was initially doubtful, but then said to myself, "Yes, I can! I'm going to take this leap of faith with Valorie." She was right! It happened that year. I got two different co-star roles. This year, Valorie's saying I'll get a guest star role. So I'm going to keep on keeping on!"* —Carolyn Faye Kramer, actor/Actor's Fast Track coach

Developing a business mindset will always mean you'll have to step out of your fear into action. That uncomfortable spot is different for everyone. All of us are more comfortable with taking some actions than others.

> *"It's been a mindset shift to look at my career as a journey. I was never doing the business Valorie teaches. I had a lot of false starts at zero because I never kept it going. It can get frustrating hoping someone will actually look at a postcard, letter, or email at the right moment. But what they end up doing with the postcards is their business. It's really gambling. I just need one casting director to align with me. The point is, acting is a journey that requires consistent action. When you take the actions, you get hired. Just be consistent and keep showing up. If you don't keep the actions going, you're always going to be starting at ground zero. Since I've been following Valorie's system for the past two years, I've been hired, I have casting directors that know me (one of them just recommended me for more work), and I've built the relationships that I need to sustain my career. I'm also getting to know the assistants who will one day become casting directors. I'm in it for the long haul."* —Brian Majestic actor/Actor's Fast Track client

DEVELOP A BUSINESS MINDSET—
What does that look like to you in your business?

VALORIE'S QUICK THOUGHTS:

- How are you procrastinating about getting out there? Be truthful. What have you really been doing? What are your excuses?

- What is your biggest fear about getting out there? Write down steps you can take to get past that fear.

- What are some negative stories you tell yourself that may be blocking you from getting out there? Write them down here. Then write down ways you can change your perception of those stories.

- List all the special talents you bring to your business as an actor and which ones of these fit the roles casting directors are seeking in your market. Why do you believe you are right for the role? Write this confident message to yourself.

- My friend and mentor Jay Perry taught me an exercise that had an incredible effect on my life. Write down 100 tolerations in your life. Then start taking them off your list one by one. What five tolerations did you list first? Start removing them from your list. Your mindset will shift as you make room for what's important.

"Nobody forced me to be an actor. No one's holding a gun to my head saying, "Brian, you must be an actor!" As a matter of fact, there are people in my life who'd prefer I wasn't one. And sometimes I've even felt that way because it meant that for all the money I've invested in my career, I could have had a great savings account or a 401K. Nobody's making me choose what is an incredibly difficult life. Or an incredibly rewarding one. I've chosen to be here. So I should be happy that I can be here, pushing forward, enjoying the ups and downs. I only booked one TV show last year but I had the best year as an actor because I no longer have any ambiguity about saying I am an actor. If you want to be a professional, whether you're ready or not, you have to jump in the deep end. Dog-paddle at first and then advance to a butterfly stroke, because eventually you're going to get good at it." —Brian Majestic actor/Actor's Fast Track client

CHAPTER 7

PLAN YOUR COMPETITIVE ADVANTAGE

Courage gives you a lifetime of happiness and freedom. And it is the main ingredient for competitive advantage.

Successful actors lean into their careers, as if precariously balanced at the edge of a balcony or canyon. They're not slouching back comfortably waiting for something to happen. It's often scary for them, but by standing out they're getting the most results.

My clients get to the top level of competitive advantage because they are consistently playing bigger than others, they are breaking rules, they're plowing through their fear and getting results. And because they are willing to go to the edge, I automatically help them. It's an earned giant fish net of access which gives them an advantage in the industry. It feels right to share that access with them.

What is meant by competitive advantage?

To illustrate what I'm talking about when I say giant fish net, recently I went to a premier for *The United States of Tara* because my friend played Toni Collette's sister on the show. Everyone was there. Wonderful catering. Stations for various personalities. Steven Spielberg. Oh, it was just beautiful.

As I stood there and glanced around the room, I could look at all the people there and say, "Oh, there's Sam Trammell. We did a movie together in '97, and then we did *True Blood* together in 2010. He's married to Missy Yaeger and she's best friends with Kate Walsh. And Kate and I did that play together in '95. I could go through the entire room that way."

Everyone was connected. It's like playing a connect-the-dots game. It's a community.

When you play at high levels, you will get high results.

Brian Majestic's story of how he got booked on *Criminal Minds* is one I want for all my clients. I told him casting director Scott David would love him. So he finally went to the casting office, located on the Quixote lot near Glendale, California, and went to the gate. The security guard asked him if he had an appointment. Brian said no, fully expecting to be told to leave his headshot folder and go. Instead, the security guard told him to wait there, went off for a moment, and came back from the casting office, saying, "Okay, go ahead." He pointed Brian in the direction of a trailer.

Brian relates the rest of the story here.

> "I walked up and Scott David was there. I said, 'Hey, I just want to drop off my headshot and resume.'" We started talking. I don't even remember what we talked about. We were just two people getting to know one other.
>
> "About a week later, I got a C-Mail notification from Actors Access. I thought, 'That's weird. I haven't submitted myself for anything. It was casting calling me in to read for this great, large co-star role.
>
> "I went in and had a terrific audition. What's interesting is I was working with a girl who said she knew the kid who got the role of my son. I remember seeing this kid's photo and realized I could never be his dad. He was a curly-haired redhead. I didn't look like him. So I was bummed out.
>
> "But I shouldn't have despaired because I got another C-Mail notice for another audition for two co-star roles. I went in that next Monday and read for three co-star roles. The following Thursday, I woke up to a voicemail from Scott David saying, 'We want to offer you a role. Congratulations! You booked it!'"

At Actor's Fast Track my coaches are all also working actors and each one of them has their own network of people. My giant fish net often intertwines with their nets because this business is such a small world.

I'm not going to sell actors on, "Hey, come work with me and you can sign with my agent. Or I know casting directors and producers." But this does happen.

My client in *Orange is the New Black* is now working with my agent. Several of my clients also work with my manager. It happens naturally, automatically. I also know a lot of agents and managers. While I don't put that out in my advertising, it is often a result of working with me. The truth is, I'm motivated to recommend someone that's on the level of competitive advantage to an agent because my vision is that we're ultimately creating a better actor for the agent. And the agent's thought is, *"Valorie is helping me out."*

The agent ends up benefitting because they get a client who will be much smarter, better prepared, and at a level of playing that's way beyond most other actors—and agents make money, which is the most important aspect for them.

Competitive advantage is when you're working within the same interconnected circle of people in a wide, significant network you want to be in. And you're in that circle because of the focused work you've done and the diligent steps you've taken to get there.

For example, director Ryan Coogler wrote and directed *Creed*. My client Mary Somers watched his movies and was quite taken with them and thought, *"I really want to be a part of what this man is doing in the industry."* I told her, *"Write him a letter."* So she sent a letter to his agent and lawyer. Then she had the opportunity to work at the LA Film Festival. She was working with a filmmaker and he asked her, *"Are you going to Ryan Coogler's talk tomorrow?"* Surprised, she said, *"Yes!"*

She had to work her day job the next day but by a miracle got her shift covered. So she ended up at Ryan Coogler's talk. The friends who had told her about it got her front-row seats for the lecture. She got to raise her hand and ask Ryan a question. Also, someone at the lecture asked him for the name of the casting director who is casting his next big movie. Mary says it was universal alignment!

The next day, I had an appointment with her and she told me what had happened. I got very excited because I have a friend of a friend who is a set designer for the production company that is producing Ryan Coogler's next movie.

Because Mary has taken the initial steps toward getting what she wants, my helping her is not just about putting my name on the line and doing somebody an arbitrary favor. Sharing my connection becomes relevant and meaningful to the steps she's already taken.

> *"In this business, entertainers are always looking for someone to throw them a bone for nothing. So operating business at the level of competitive advantage is very different because when you take those important, consistent steps, you earn that hand up."* —Mary Somers actor/Actor's Fast Track client

At Actor's Fast Track, we have the experience to give actors advice based on my 32+ years of acting and work with thousands of actors (what works, what doesn't work, and what has the tendency to work better). But I also must be watchful I don't pass along my own fear around something. When I catch myself doing that, I have to pull back and say, "Okay. Is that **my** fear?"

My coaches are trained that we don't "fix" our actors. Rather, we give them action steps.

The **only** way to gain an edge over others is to put yourself out there in front in ways that may be hard for you or unconventional. Get out of your comfort zone, think outside the box, and develop the business acumen and skills beyond acting that separate you from the crowd. Network: Start meeting people, shake hands, and introduce yourself.

Talent can only take you so far; you must be savvy and do the rest. **Show up in the room with who you're becoming, not with who you are.** Act as though you're already successful.

> *"By being part of the Actor's Fast Track community, I've just signed with an agent I'm really happy about. Plus, at our bi-weekly phone calls, it's good to know everyone's going through the same things. I don't feel so alone doing it. For example, I went to a meeting with a management company and felt very strong. I'd just come from work on Adolescence but they said "no" because I didn't have any television credits. That "no" really stung because I went in feeling so confident. I was having a hard time springing back and it was nice to get support. For me, the Actor's Fast Track community eliminates all of the "noise", the self-doubt, thinking about the future, being wrapped up in the result of "I want it now." It helps me keep on the grind and accountable."* —Courtney Bandeko actor/Actor's Fast Track client

Getting uncomfortable nets results.

Recently, I read some testimonials about a very big career coach. All the testimonials raved about how great the actors felt about themselves and how great they felt about their careers. The truth is, my actors don't always feel great. What they have to do is hard.

But it's also true that in the past three years I've had clients go from no credits to starring in a Sony feature. Three clients got recurring roles on TV series and tons of clients booked single roles in films, TV, and theatre. WHY?

Because they are out on the edge. While being on the edge can be uncomfortable, scary, emotional, downright crazy-making, and not always a great feeling, this is how you get a career and move into competitive advantage. That's also how you're going to get work.

When you're playing at a higher level, you will get high results. These people have really staked their flag in the sand and made a clear claim for who they are—and they've stuck by it. Now they've started to get paid. Not everyone reaches competitive advantage, and no one gets to competitive advantage without having really started to book the work.

> *"Being part of the Actor's Fast Track community inspires me to keep moving and motivates me to do more."*—Ana Maria Perez actor/Actor's Fast Track client)

What I'm trying to get you, the actor, to do is flow. Competitive advantage is a flow. Most actors are guilty of stop-and-start or part-time endeavors. Or they're playing in the wrong ball park because they're doing things that have nothing to do with selling.

It's all selling. But once you get beyond the word, *selling* you get to *serving*. This is where the magic comes alive. Then you understand how to have a competitive advantage, which means YOU'RE IN.

> *"Mindset alone is not enough. The great part about all of it is the partnership between mindset, strategy, and community. Community is at its best when mindset is addressed."*—Belanie Dishong, Live at Choice

Some clients come to me with great opportunities already in place but don't necessarily know how to leverage them. One of my VIP clients, for example, has a best friend who is very involved the industry. Because of this, my client participates in events with amazingly connected people. Most of my other clients would kill for that kind of opportunity. But her issue is learning how to garner all the information from people at these events and turn them into buyers. She's blown a few truly great opportunities, but she's learning from her mistakes.

For an example of someone who *is* living in competitive advantage, look to Bryan Coffee. He's the Metro PCS guy on TV and has been on two sitcoms.

He ended up on the Disney set for an entire week because his friend was a writer on the show. The Executive Producer is a friend of mine, one of my biggest fans at Disney. Bryan shared that he and I are connected with the Executive Producer. The next thing you know, Bryan got an audition for the show.

He shares the full story here.

> "Due to working with Valorie, she recommended I talk to producer/writer Jim O'Doherty. He does a lot of Disney shows.
>
> "So, I did a little research on him and found out he was writing on a show that an old acquaintance and friend of mine was writing on with him. I contacted my friend through Facebook just to say hello and congratulations and to tell him I was looking for Jim O'Doherty.
>
> "My friend said, 'Hey, it's so good to talk with you. I haven't talked with you in so long! Why don't you come down to the set, hang out and meet everybody? I'll lead you around and share them.'
>
> "I said, "Definitely!" I was blown away because that really wasn't what I was asking; I was just saying congratulations, I know this business is tough, I'm glad you're working.
>
> "About a week and a half later, I went down to the set with a bunch of cannoli and a bottle of whiskey for my friend. And he showed me around. I got to meet everybody. And the casting director just happened to be there that day.

> "When I left the studio, I called my manager and said, 'This is something I just did.' And she said, 'You know, there's a part on that show I think you should go in for. It's perfect for you.' So she said, 'Let me call them right now.'
>
> "The very next day, I was in for an audition for a part. In less than two weeks, it went from suggestion to audition. That was probably the fastest turnaround for networking that I've ever had. It was **awesome**.
>
> "As a result of that audition, I got to sit and talk with the casting directors for 15 minutes. This seldom happens. You usually go in, do your part, and leave. But because they came to me in a very unusual way, they wanted to know who I was. I got to sit and talk with them. We had common connections, which was even better.
>
> "For me, this was an entirely new way to make a contact and get in there, and combined with having a manager and being able to communicate with her and get in that way, I was able to use both sides of the coin.
>
> "The season was nearly over, and I didn't get the part. So it's my educated guess that they just wanted to meet me. But I did make some very valuable contacts, and now there's interest for the future. I'm part of a community. When the show comes back again next year, I'm going to contact Brian and post what's going on with me."

My client, Carolyn Faye Kramer, is also in competitive advantage. She and I are also inexorably intertwined. She just booked *Diary of Anne Frank* at the Olney Theatre, which is a huge job, and Pat McCorkle cast her in that show. Interestingly, Pat McCorkle also cast me in *The Crucible* at The Roundabout Theatre. That connectedness is the cornerstone of competitive advantage.

Carolyn explains how Actor's Fast Track supports her career and gives her competitive advantage.

> "You can come to a call when you've had a terrible audition and ask people, 'Have you met this casting director before?' There's amazing support, comradery, and a push to be better because you're seeing people around you taking risks. Also, if you're scared, you can reach out and people will rally around you and let you know you'll be fine.

"When you're on an Actor's Fast Track accountability call, you hear what everyone's doing. This person made a cold call. That person got a callback or an audition. It causes you to think, 'Jeez, I need to work harder!' You're seeing other people do it so you know you can do it too.

"Other people can be great resources, too, such as providing you with the addresses of casting offices. Someone will say, 'Oh, I've been there. I just made a drop-off to that casting office.' They'll tell you where to do your drop-off, who to talk to, or how to get past security. We're here to support each other. The cool thing about Valorie is she's pushed all of us to find out what our type is. So, you can find something specific about you so there's no competition even if you are the same demographic, ethnicity and age-range as someone else."

In the Actor's Fast Track community, it's invaluable to have a group of people you can draw on for help who have your back and support you when you're doing well and when you're not doing well.

Being an actor can be very isolating. The industry can also create a lot of competition. But here, even if you're the same type as someone else, you're not in competition with them. Everyone lifts everyone else up. Essentially, when you're in competitive advantage you naturally become part of a community of successful, connected people.

The greatest thing about Actor's Fast Track is the power of my community. My actors are **so** smart and brave. And they're all getting auditions and signing with agents and booking BIG things. It's crazy! I'm surrounded by successful actors.

"The more specific you are, the more you're in competitive advantage. This seems counter-intuitive because you want people to know your range for all kinds of roles. But it's how it works." —Carolyn Faye Kramer actor/Actor's Fast Track client.

Sara Banerjee also describes how the Actor's Fast Track community helps her stay in competitive advantage:

> "Being a part of Valorie's very tight network is like "five degrees of Kevin Bacon." Someone who knows someone, who knows someone, who knows someone, who knows someone might get you your next job. You never know. It's all about building relationships and connections. Being a part of the Actor's Fast Track community "lights a fire under your ass!" Whenever you feel like you're lagging and getting down on yourself and connect with others in the network, you take action. It gets you moving again.
>
> "You hear what everyone else is doing and their trials and tribulations. It's a very empathetic space because everyone else gets what you're going through. You can nurse your wounds and be encouraged. It's a place to be seen, heard, and to put it all out there. It also bumps you to get off your ass, stay in the game, be active, and go for the gold because everyone else is taking action. It's great because the days you don't want to be doing something, you just call up your coach or post something on the website and someone will convince you to take some kind of action for that day if you haven't done your five actions for the week.

> "The biggest gift Valorie has given me is I know someone has faith in me. I've never met anyone who believes in my dream the same way I see it. She believes in my career. I didn't think I was ready. I was being told I would grow into my type in a few years. She gave me the understanding that there is no moment of readiness. You don't know if you can fly until you jump. And that's an invaluable part of her coaching." —Mary Somers actor/Actor's Fast Track client

DEVELOPING COMPETITIVE ADVANTAGE: TOP TEN THINGS I WANT YOU TO KNOW

1. **Knowledge is power.** The more you know about your industry, the better: names, projects, literally everything that's happening. All knowledge is power. Read Huffington Post, listen to NPR, have an opinion, know what is going on in the world.

2. **Know your craft and love it!** It makes you sexier.

3. **Look like you've already arrived.** Wear nicely-made, fashionable clothes. Be on trend. Know your marketability.

4. **Be honest and sincere.** Come from a place of gratitude. Give back. Pay it forward. It's the circle of life.

5. **Don't be greedy.**

6. **Build a team of support from the very beginning to get you where you want to go.** The team mentality is the right way to think! Don't go it alone!!!

7. **Know what you want and where you are going.** Be able to talk eloquently about that.

8. **Have some money.** You're going to need it.

9. **Make a list and keep track of who you meet and everything you know about these people.** This is how you create an empire.

10. **Live a full life! Have a blast!** (I have.)

PLAN YOUR COMPETITIVE ADVANTAGE—
How close to the edge are you willing to go?

VALORIE'S BONUS THOUGHTS:

- How much do you know about your industry: names, projects, and literally everything that's happening? Write it down.
- What are ways you can go beyond selling to serving in your career to build business connections and quality of life?
- Are you guilty of stop-and-start or part-time endeavors? What are steps you can take to commit to acting full-time?
- Are you playing in the wrong ball park because you're not selling yourself to buyers?
- Have you staked a claim and made it clear that you know who you are? If yes, describe who can benefit from who you are and want to book you.
- Who is your network people and what steps can you take to expand your net?
- What does "being out on the edge" (scary actions) look like in your business? List three ways you can push yourself out there even further.
- Can you think of times in your career when you have showed up in the room as if you had already arrived? How did it help your business?

CHAPTER 8

OVERCOMING THE TEN OBSTACLES ALL ACTORS FACE

After working with hundreds of actors, I've realized there are common ways they get in their own way. All of these tend to be based in self-created mistruths.

I'm including the top ten mind shifts we use at Actor's Fast Track to ensure our clients are in the right mindset to succeed. These principles can help launch your business in the direction you want it to go, too. Remember, to get new results, you'll need to apply new methods.

TOP TEN MIND SHIFTS FOR ACTORS

1 There are a million ways to get there.

There's always a different way to do something other than the one that's not working for you. There's never just one way to do anything. There's **always** an escape hatch, a different tunnel. Don't stop looking. If you are doggedly determined because you're unwilling to compromise on what you want your life to look like, then you will not stop.

There's always another hall. Turn around! Be open to the possibilities. Ask yourself, *"Is there another way I could do this? Do I have to do it this way?"*

Often what we **think** we also have to do stops us from doing it. For example, actors often tell themselves *"I need to get an agent to have a career."*

They will wait to start their career until they have that perfect agent. It's not necessary! I had my first perfect agent eleven years into my career, with big plays under my belt. Actors can get stopped by believing there's only one way to do things.

For instance, if an actor comes up to me and says *"I want to be on Justified."* I'll say, *"Great. Go get on Justified."*

Then a year later, I find them and ask, *"So how was that getting on Justified?"*

And they say, *"Well, I thought to get on Justified, I needed an agent. Oh, wait, before I got an agent, I needed a reel. And so on_____"*

So, for the last year, they've been stuck in *"I need to get a reel, so I'm not getting onto Justified."*

I say, *"Why didn't you just go knock on the door of Graham Yost, the creator of Justified?"* What is the harm in that?

And their answer is, *"Oh, I never thought of that."* They've been told this is the way you have to do things. And it's just not true.

Most of the time what I tell my coaches is, *"Did you look for a different way for them? Did you try this, or did you try that?"* That is what we are always working on at Actor's Fast Track—looking at creative, imaginative ways to find new solutions.

So when you start thinking there is only one way to do something, stop thinking that way! Always look for another approach. It's there and often even better than your original plan.

2. There are many nos on the road to yes.

So many actors get stopped by **one** no. The truth is, you're going to collect a lot of nos to get that final yes.

Some actors can get turned down for years. And it's very disheartening. But generally, if you have been told no for years, there are probably some things you can learn at Actor's Fast Track to turn those responses into yeses.

Having said that, I believe if you are putting yourself out solidly, clearly and concisely for one year, you're going to get somewhere. But you are going to get told no a lot.

And when you get told no, you may wail, "But I am so amazing! And I have this great stance."

My advice is to stand strong with your flag planted in the ground and be true to who you are—because there will be people all around you telling you to change. And then all the energy you should be using to get YOU out there will be spent in trying to change yourself. It won't work.

Stay the path. And expect to see no, no, no, no, no, no, no, all the way to YES!

Actors don't get picked. But that's not because they're not worthy of being chosen.

How you make a million dollars is you do that thing that works over and over again repetitively until you're bored with it. So be steadfast and unwavering in your goal.

Don't let just one no stop you. If you're one of the many actors who gets stopped by one no, just realize you'll be told no multiple times before you get a yes. It's part of the job.

For instance, I was at a benefit one night and Ed Norton and Mary Louise Parker were there. I was sitting at the table with two actresses, and one actress said to the other that she never had a career because she couldn't figure that agent game out because thirty years earlier an agent she thought was going to sign her didn't. This actress got stuck for 30 years due to **one no**!

It made me think, oh my god, what if *I* had been stopped by times I was told no? Those crushing refusals scared the heck out of me at the time. But I didn't let them stop me.

3 You hold the key to open your own doors.

Don't wait for the industry to give you permission to enter the marketplace or for when you're "good enough." Too many actors are waiting to be invited in. That elusive invitation is just not going to arrive in the mail.

Actors often think an agent is going to come along and tell them who they're going to be and what they're going to do and how they're going to do it. But as I've mentioned in previous chapters, that's just not true.

You have to come from your **own** point of view and build that vision. Create your "whatever-you-want-to-be" and boldly put it out there.

If you see yourself as a philanthropic Mark Wahlberg kind of guy, then do charitable projects you care about and get a strong support system around you to deliver your message. Then you can become known for who you are: a caring and involved person.

At my workshops, I always do a little skit where I'm standing outside of a party and I say to an actor, *"Hi. How are you? I'm going to the party. Are you going to the party?"*

Then this guy saunters right by us and goes directly into the party. HEY! He just went right into the party! How did he do that!? Pure and simple. He did it by just walking right in.

So don't wait for the industry to invite you in. You don't need anyone's permission. Just walk in.

4. What have you done for me lately? Bring buyers what they need.

Actors tend to show up hat in hand with nothing to give in return. Rather than ask what others can do for you, think instead about what you can do for them. Don't just say, *"Gimme, gimme, gimme."* Think like a business person.

Instead of complaining about not getting auditions or waiting for that big break, be of service to your career, your agent, and your scene partner. Don't ask them, "What have you done for me?" Rather, say, "Here's what I can do for you." Be clear about what you're selling and then offer it to them.

When you show up to buyers, know what your value is, whether it's trackable through your conversion rate (how many auditions it takes for you to get a callback) or how many mailings it takes for you to get an answer to emails or drop-offs. Be ready to say, *"I am worth this."* Get a little too big for your britches!

Remember, you're there as an actor to help your buyers make money.

5 You manage your own impression and legacy.

You control how other people think of you. You are the contractor of your career. So go build! No one is going to give your career to you.

It's your life. You leave a legacy from the time you're born, including what people think about you depending on how you treated them throughout your life. How you measure that is through the majority's perception of you. You create how you are seen.

For example, what is your perception of O.J. Simpson? There was a split decision in 1995 regarding his innocence and guilt for the murder of his wife, Nicole Brown Simpson, and her friend Ron Goldman. But as his reputation began to crumble and the veneer of his personality cracked, even those who supported him in the beginning began to realize the likelihood of his guilt. Now, twenty years later, it's pretty clear to most people that his lawyers used perfect social and political timing to manipulate the outcome of his verdict and that he was most likely guilty. His legacy is now completely tarnished. Plus, he's serving time—a very long time—for an unrelated crime: armed robbery.

Everyone also thinks Britney Spears is a cuckoo-potamous because she shaved her head in the middle of paparazzi. We all watched her shave her head and show her va-jay-jay to the camera because she chose to do that. No matter how much she comes back, that will always be a Scarlet Letter for her because she created it in the public eye. She has a great career but she's still a cuckoo-potamous. She did that to herself.

In contrast, everyone in this town loves Reese Witherspoon.

Recently Reese was honored at a ball in Beverly Hills and she greeted all 250 guests personally at the door. The gesture was so beautiful that when I heard about it, it made me cry with respect. Her reputation in the Hollywood community is so good. And she's made that happen.

She's the one who's learned everyone's name on set. She's the one who writes thank you notes to people. And **she's** the one who has created herself as lovable. No one did this for her.

George Clooney is the same way. There are so many great, wonderful actors who are doing so much more for the world than acting.

We've been the jesters of the world for centuries, ever since there have been clowns. It's what we do. But I think we're doing much more now.

Actors are giving back to the world and really trying to help people.

The crux is how do you want to be seen? This is BIG. It's about your reputation, vision, manifestation, implementation—and ultimately, your legacy.

6. Don't go check in with the herd (other actors, acting teachers, friends, family) because all you'll get is the "well, I heard…"

This one is my personal favorite because I imagine all these cows on a hill and they've all been congregating there for years. They're mooing, *"I've been an actor for seven years and I've tried everything."* Or the teacher cow that used to be an actor is standing on a mound, bellowing, *"Well, you can't really make it in this business."* The cows are all there, chewing their cud.

You're a frisky calf and you bound up enthusiastically, saying, *"Hey, I was thinking it might be a good idea if I made some cookies and took them to this casting director!"*

The naysayer cows all turn to look at you, snorting disparagingly, *"Well, I heard if you take the cookies they'll yell at you and you could actually even get arrested."* Or, *"I HEARD…."*

So, with your enthusiasm dampened, you don't do it and quietly join the herd. You may even start talking to yourself in negative "cow-speak," *moo…boo…boo.*

My advice? Don't go check in with those cows! Don't listen to them. Don't let them put those thoughts in your head so you start doubting yourself. There is no need to check in with them. Instead, check in with a good guide like Actor's Fast Track because we will say, "Go do it, my child. You should just go do it!" Because that is what we are about.

We're a supportive community that won't discourage you from breaking the rules. We won't listen to your excuses. The most exciting thing about my company is the community that's occurred. They are so different from any other acting community.

Get out of that herd mentality which will talk you out of doing what you want to do.

Actors are notorious for asking their actor friends what they should do or think. These same friends don't have a credit on their resume.

Therefore, if you want to go and do a drop-off to an agent's office, don't ask your friends. They will tell you, "Oh, you're not supposed to do that" or "My friend went to an agency and they yelled at her." Also, don't check in with your family or your acting teachers who don't have an active career or never have had an active career about what you should do with your business.

Don't listen the "HEARDS." Let your impulse design your action. Genius is inspiration. Fear motivates the "HEARD." The herd will always hate the right action. They're ALWAYS going to tell you not to take the big risk. **The big risk is what's going to get you the job.**

7. Go beyond your fear curtain.

What are you afraid of exactly? Is the casting director going to bite you? Not like you? Are they going to yell at you?

Really. GET DOWN TO IT.

The first thing you need to do is determine what big action you want to take. What is that thing you're thinking of doing that you've told yourself you can't do? Such as, *"Oh, I'm thinking of calling Leonardo DiCaprio."*

What scares you about it? What is he going to say? *"You're a fricking terrible person for calling me. I don't want to talk to you and don't ever call me again!"* If he does say that, can you live with it?

But of course, even as I'm writing that possibility, I know he's not going to say that. Why would he? You share a passion for the same craft he does. You can offer something to him, such as, *"I'm Valorie Hubbard. I want to know you and play your mother. I want you to see what I've done. Can I send you my stuff?"*

Why can't I do that!?

I just took you over my own fear curtain. That's the best way I can show you what I mean. Most of our fears are unfounded. They're stupid! When you say them out loud, you go, *"Okay, come on! How can I be scared of that? It makes no sense."*

I mean, what could be the worst thing that would happen if Leonardo said to me, *"Are you flipping crazy? No effing way!"* It's not as though it's going to ruin my life, even if he did. But he just wouldn't.

Of course, you have to know that what you're bringing to the conversation is worthwhile and what you're offering to Leonardo can help him before making that call.

But you can call him if you know going into the phone call that what you're offering is genuinely positive and beneficial to him. You know you're not just calling with your hat in hand asking for a handout. This belief in yourself gives you courage to actually make the call.

Going through this process and experiencing your greatest fear puts it into perspective. Actually writing about it in this book makes me realize right now where I'm blocked.

When Kristy Staky booked her role on *Switched at Birth*, I asked her, "What's the worst thing that can happen? That Dee Dee Bradley says, *"How dare you send me a fricking video on my Facebook page! You're an idiot!"* or *"You'll never work as an actress!"* Can you live with that? Yes? Well, then just go do it!"

> *"Valorie has taught me how to be self-confident and believe in myself. But for almost a year, I didn't do anything she told me to do. I didn't contact casting directors because I'd go to casting workshops and hear them say, "Don't submit anything directly." But Valorie would say, "Go, go, go!" And, oh my god, I was so scared. I didn't know what their reaction would be. And then I finally did it—and it worked! After my first drop-off, I got called in for a studio pilot, a leading role, and went straight to the producer session."* —Ana Maria Perez, actor/Actor's Fast Track client

8. Lucky breaks take a lot of consistent work.

If I could only find that magic pill to solve all my problems, book that perfect role, and find a great agent. Well, this isn't going to happen unless you win the lottery or you're Alice in Wonderland. Also, even those chance windfalls often cause more problems than solutions.

There is no such thing as a "lucky break." That's a crock of nonsense.

Luck is a lifestyle choice. The journey is a flow. Andrew Bachelor did not get lucky. He worked for it. He posted three Vines a day. He was consistent.

I had a young man over here last night. He's going to be a megastar! Many people want to leap ahead when they're not ready. So, when he started looking at publicists, I said, "Okay, I have a recommendation." But just to be sure, I checked with him first, asking, "How's your structure doing?" Because you have to build that Noah's Ark, baby, before heading out into the waves.

The magic in your life and career will happen due to a lifestyle of regularly nurturing relationships, having product materials ready all the time, working your craft, reaching out, creating your own opportunities, and having an attitude of gratitude and excitement.

9. Get, use, and grow your support base.

Here's what happens: People get excited about their career, they do something like hire me or go to acting school, and then they end up hiding or giving up. They start and then stop. Star and start again. Start. Stop. Change. Stop. There's no fluidity to their business. There's no flow.

I represent one idea: me. And there's just so far my own mind can take me. But if I am in a community of successful people, they can help me be more successful because their views will help me grow. Don't stop growing!

Seek out the people who have done what you want to do. GET the resources they used. An exercise bike is worthless without a rider. So USE the resources you put in place. Ask for help, attend meetings, show up for support, and it will show up for YOU. GROW, NURTURE, and SURROUND yourself with people to help you build your support base.

10. What if your acting career were a matter of life or death?

What if you **had** to make a living acting? If you've been paying attention in this book, by now you know part-time actors only get part-time results.

But if you had to be working as an actor full-time, the first thing you would do is take stock of your situation and then show up. This is not a hobby!

If you're starting a company to pay the rent and want this business to deliver a living to you, then you'd better give it "living" attention. Become non-negotiable and this acting career becomes non-negotiable.

WHAT ARE YOU WAITING FOR? WHAT EXACTLY DO YOU THINK IS GOING TO HAPPEN?

The scourge of most actors is that they are part-time actors and they're thinking that means if they play at the semi-amateur ballgame then they'll be able to play with the Yankees. The actual truth is that they have no connection. They will never leave the semi-amateur ball field. You have to play with the big boys *before you're ready* to play with the big boys—and show up as a smart business person.

In my workshops, I use what I call The Fear Clock to chart fears common to actors. It's likely you'll see some familiar themes from your own life when you consider the following fears we all face and can learn to overcome:

THE FEAR	THE SOLUTION
I am too old.	Change your point of view. (Melissa Leo and Margot Martindale won big in their 50s.)
I didn't go to the right school.	So what? Neither did Johnny Depp.
I am not pretty/handsome enough.	Start there!! You are selling you, so you'd better like what you're selling.
I'm going to suck.	YEP. That's how we all learn.
I don't have enough money!	Yes, you need capital to start a business, but spend it wisely and get some guidance and help. Keep your eye on the prize.
I won't be able to get an agent.	And THAT'S OKAY. If you are moving towards what you want, the right agent will come at the right time.

I am too FAT.	SELL WHAT YOU HAVE!!
What if they don't like me?	Some people are going to like you and some people are not. And vice versa.
I don't know anybody famous.	Go meet someone connected today, set that intention, and the next thing you know, you will know EVERYONE.
I'm not good enough.	Michael Chekov said it took 20 years to become a good actor. It's the journey; give it a chance.
It's going to be a scary ride.	YEP! SO BUCKLE UP YOUR SEAT BELT.

Remember, it's your career and no one else's. Not your mother's, your father's, or your agent's career. It is your career.

> *"In the acting community, I often see competition. What Valorie is developing is a genuine support community which isn't based on "if I do for you, you do for me" but on the pure sense of encouragement, helping one another. It's incredible to watch her bring those people into sharing the producers, directors, managers and all the people that they come to know—they share with each other! She's really changing the world and acting business for actors. This is a whole new, young group coming in. And I think we're going to see, coupled with the mindset work, a community of actors that are standing in their own self-endorsement."* —Belanie Dishong, Live at Choice)

Top Ten Mind Shifts for Actors— what's in your mind?

VALORIE'S PARTING LAST MINUTE THOUGHTS:

- What must you do that is currently stopping you from getting out there?
- If you could have it your way, how would it go?
- Think of the no responses you've received along the way. How did you react to them and what did you do about it?
- What are ways you've opened your own doors in the past? List some ways you could open more of them in the future.
- Think of ways you can be of service to your career and your agent, manager, scene partner(s) and community. List them here.
- List actions you can take to build an ethical business reputation.
- What have you heard the "herd" say which might be stopping you?
- What fears do you have on the Fear Clock? How do you plan to start telling yourself new positive stories about these fears?
- List the people who have done what you want to do. Get the resources they used.
- Ask yourself if your acting career is non-negotiable. If it is, list here what you plan to do to give it "living attention."

THAT'S ALL FOLKS!

Thank you for reading my book. The curtain is closing now on this show. If you're interested in joining my tribe or having me walk with you down your career path, I would love to talk. As an actor, you're an entrepreneur. It's hard to build a business by yourself, so feel free to email me at Valorie@actorsfasttrack.com and I'll be in touch. I'd love to help you in your journey to success.
I'll see you out there on the edge!

    My clients/coaches selflessly donated their time, creative energy and perspective to the success of this book. They are my wonderful Guest Stars—and my heartfelt thanks go out to all of them.

PLAYBILL

CAST: IN ORDER OF APPEARANCE

Mary Somers: (*The bad girl, werewolf girlfriend and edgy, bitchy girl with an attitude. She's a little rough around the edges and doesn't give a crap.*)

Mary Somers knew she wanted to become an actor when she was three years old. As a child growing up in Russia, she learned to speak English watching Rogers and Hammerstein movies. While watching Oklahoma, she realized she wanted to act. So upon coming to the states, she studied dance, moving into acting. She's best known for her roles as Poppy Love in *12*, and as a dinner guest in *The Possessed Waiter*.

Brian Majestic: (*The blue-collar, every man who can survive in the woods without a hatchet: a police officer, detective, or best friend to the lead; one of the guys. You want him to arrive on the scene because he's a stabilizing force, the guy who's going to take charge and make sure everything is okay.*)

Brian Majestic was born in Pittsburgh, Pennsylvania, to Maureen (Majestic) and Robert M. Seuffert. At seven years of age, he began studying tap, jazz, and ballet. His first stage appearance was as a Jet in *West Side Story* at Byham Theatre, Pittsburgh. He booked work in plays and musicals in Pittsburgh before moving to New York City, where he attended the American Academy of Dramatic Arts. In the fall of 2001, Brian placed his artistic career on hold to enlist in the United States Marine Corps. He served seven years as a Field Radio Operator with two combat deployments to Iraq. Upon completion of his enlistment, Brian moved to Los Angeles to pursue TV/film acting.

Recent credits include work on *Criminal Minds, Close Your Eyes Slow, Dinosaur Bullets, Replaced, Hostage Do or Die, Solo: The Series, Elevator, Night of the Zombie King, The Best Friend, The Unit,* and *Extraction.*

Esme Bañuelos—*(The Hispanic Latina action star; the next Angelina Jolie or Michelle Rodriquez. She's a tough friend; there when a boy gives you trouble. Friends can count on her.)*

Esme Banuelos was born in Wichita, Kansas. The eldest of her siblings in a large Mexican family, from the time Esme first performed as a child in the role of a tree, to *The Crucible* in high school, to now, Esme has always been drawn to acting. She attended Wichita State University, where she earned a Bachelor in Performing Arts and certificate in film. With three callbacks to the Hulu show, *East Los* and a tape for *Chicago Med already on her resume,* she is unstoppable.

Carolyn Faye Kramer—*(A young James Adams meets Timmy Schmidt with a pop of Minnie Driver. Also. a young Carol Kane or Geraldine Hughes. The hardworking nursing resident who's holding the family together, caring for her disabled grandparents.)*

In addition to many roles on New York and Chicago stages, Carolyn Faye Kramer is known for her work in (television) *The Family, LFE* and (film) *Sunshine Away, In Memoriam, Girl Parts, Adam Bloom, Blonde Moments, Locked, Holding Cell,* and *The Picnic.* She also holds a First-Degree Black Belt in Kung Fu and speaks a number of dialects: British (RP & Cockney), Irish, Romanian, French, American Southern, New York, and old Jewish men from Boston.

CAST: In order of appearance

Courtney Bandeko—(*A young, greasy, homeless, runaway delinquent kid with a tattoo*)

Courtney Bandeko is best known for her work in *Adolescence, Slash* and *Southbound*. She has also had roles in the indie comedy *Pacific Northwest* and the indie psychological thriller, *Circle*. Plus, she stars in *Gilt*, produced by the Ironwood Gang, featuring Christina Milian. Courtney is currently studying at Lonsdale-Smith Studios with Michèle Lonsdale-Smith, Chekhov Studio International with Marjo-Riikka Makela, and Second City, Hollywood.

Sara Banerjee—(*A witty Indian or Asian girl doctor or lawyer*)

Ever since she was child in the San Francisco Bay Area in San Jose, California, Sara Banerjee has been passionate about acting and dancing. She grew up watching Bollywood movies and used to dance around the living room in costume with her mom. After moving to Los Angeles, she obtained a doctorate in physical therapy. And when this work didn't inspire her the way acting had, she returned to her professional acting career. Sara is best known for her work in *Cesar Chavez, The Lost Michelle Obama Tapes: Tape Number One—The Sermon on the Mount According to Michelle Obama*, and *American Blend*.

Bryan Coffee—(*Comedic guy*)—Actor, Writer, Director Bryan Coffee was born in Syosset, New York, USA. He lives in Los Angeles with his wife, Ann Bowman. Byan has played comedic support on TV shows including *MONK, iCarly, Suburgatory, RAKE, Stevie TV, Blue Collar TV* and HBO's *The Brink*. He's done commercials on camera and voice-over, written several group Sketch Comedy shows, and created and performed his own one-man show, *The Brink of Extinction*.

He also founded and performs with *Ten West,* an ensemble dedicated to creating and performing cutting-edge, original shows which take a humorous look at human experience. *Ten West's* multi-disciplinary style, with a strong emphasis on non-verbal physical comedy, educates and creates shows for youth, exploring vital life skills such as conflict-resolution, character and good manners. Bryan is most known for his work on *Kevin From Work, Side Effects, How I Saved the World, The Bogus Witch Project,* and *The Bellman.*

Ana Maria Perez—*(Edgy, exotic woman)*

Ana Maria Perez is a producer and actress, known for *City of Dead Men* (2014), *Pasos de Héroe* (2016) and *A Mano Limpia* (2010). Film credits also include *Bang, Hysteria 212,* and *The Sun Always Shines Letting You Go.* Additional performances include *Amor en Custodia (television),* and *Glass Menagerie, Fool for Love, Hatful of Rain, My Friend Never Said Goodbye,* and *The Dreamer Examines His Pillow (Theatre*.) Educated at the Lee Strasberg Theatre and Film Institute, Los Angeles, she  is tri-lingual in Spanish, English, and Italian. She also versed in the following dialects: Spanish, Mexican, Argentinian, Italian.

Belanie Dishong—*(CEO-Live at Choice)* Belanie Dishong works with many Actor's Fast Track clients in Los Angeles and New York. She successfully helps them identify, hone and change their mindset. Founder and CEO of *Live at Choice, Live at Choice Media* and the *Starfisher Academy of Coaches,* Belanie is an author, keynote speaker, course leader, personal coach and radio talk show host. She leads people to self-discovery, and helps them transform their beliefs so they can make new choices for success. Through her Live at Choice, Beyond Circumstances, Mastery of the Script and Unpainted Picture programs, Belanie helps others achieve extraordinary lives. We love the work she does with our actors!

ABOUT THE AUTHOR

Valorie Hubbard owns the company, Actor's Fast Track, where she consults with working actors about their career paths. Having navigated her own career, she knows the pitfalls and successes of the path and how to avoid the one and create the other. She gives actors the tools they need to get recognized.

Her first book, *The Actors Workbook: how to become a working actor*, published by Allyn Amp Bacon Publishers, co-written with Lea Tolub-Brandenberg, teaches readers how to transition from student acting to professional work. Lively and engaging, the book also gives educators content for teaching.

In her newest book, *Rule Breakers: Changing the Way Actors Do Business*, she shows professional actors how to create and operate their acting career as a successful business—and how to move from being "stuck" into the limelight.

Valorie was born to act. Her first starring performance was at the age of three when, much to the dismay of her mother, she dramatically threw herself down a staircase—and she's has been acting ever since. Attending The Goodman School of Drama, she spent 20 years performing in New York. Notable favorite credits there include *The Crucible* at The Roundabout Theatre, *The Country Boy* at Irish Rep and *The Sweepers* and *The Queen Bee & #39's Last Stand* at Urban Stages.

Also performing in the New Jersey Shakespeare Festival, Delaware Theatre Company, The Wilma Theatre, Weston Playhouse, Missouri Rep and The Lab Theatre in Poland, Valorie was a member of the last international company to work at the Lab Theatre. She's also collaborated with an amazing range of acting professionals including John Guare, Joseph Chaiken, Toni Kotite, Neel Keller, Terry Schreiber and Zbigniew Cynkutis.

About the Author

Moving to Los Angeles 10 years ago, Valorie launched into screen. Film credits include *Sex, Death and Bowling; Trigger; A Better Life; An American Christmas Carol; Divorce Invitation; The Hannah Montana Movie; Smell of Success; Pennance; Resident Evil: Extinction; Parasomnia; Henry Fool; Wrestling with Alligators; Gameday;* and the Hallmark Christmas movie *Help for the Holidays.*

TV Credits include roles on *Castle, Agent & #39's of S.H.I.E.L.D; How I Met Your Mother; Glee; American Horror Story; Workaholics; True Blood; 90210; ER; Desperate Housewives; The Middle; Zeke and Luther; Good Luck Charlie; I'm in the Band;* a recurring role on *Kickin It and General Hospital; HUGE; The Job; Missing Persons; Comedy Central &#39's; American Body Shop* and *Chocolate News.* She also plays the "hot" Rhonda in the recent release of video game *Dead Rising 3.*

Valorie lives in Los Angeles with her husband Chef Gill Boyd and dog Gracie

Made in the USA
San Bernardino, CA
11 October 2018